# Havoc-06

## A Combat Controller On Operations

Troy Knight
With Brooke Strahan

16pt

# Copyright Page from the Original Book

Copyright © Troy Knight

First published 2021

This book is copyright. Apart from any fair dealing for the purposes of private study, research, criticism or review as permitted under the Copyright Act, no part may be reproduced, stored in a retrieval system or transmitted in any form or by any means, electronic, mechanical, photocopying, recording or otherwise, without written permission.

All inquiries should be made to the publishers.

Big Sky Publishing Pty Ltd
PO Box 303, Newport, NSW 2106, Australia
Phone: 1300 364 611
Fax: (61 2) 9918 2396
Email: info@bigskypublishing.com.au
Web: www.bigskypublishing.com.au

Cover design and typesetting: Think Productions

A catalogue record for this book is available from the National Library of Australia

Title: HAVOC-06, A Combat Controller on Operations

## TABLE OF CONTENTS

| | |
|---|---|
| FOREWORD: Murray Turner | i |
| FOREWORD: Dan Schilling | v |
| AUTHOR'S NOTE: by Brooke Strahan | ix |
| AUTHOR'S NOTE: by Troy Knight | xii |
| To my children | xvii |
| To my fallen mates | xviii |
| INTRODUCTION: Norm, Norm, but Different | xix |
| 1: A Dirty RAAFie | 1 |
| 2: Lantana | 16 |
| 3: Nitro Circus, Iraq | 27 |
| 4: Schulzy | 35 |
| 5: Up Close and Personal | 47 |
| 6: A Very Pleasant Cruise | 53 |
| 7: Contracted | 61 |
| 8: The Murder of Darren Hoare | 86 |
| 9: Pirates and Kiwis and Seals, Oh my! | 96 |
| 10: Nasi Goreng | 106 |
| 11: Selected | 119 |
| 12: Fuck it, We Are Going Live! | 129 |
| 13: Walking the Blue Pipeline | 140 |
| 14: Red Dust Beginnings | 149 |
| 15: Fuckery and 500-Pounders | 155 |
| 16: Luck of the Irish, but I'm not Irish | 169 |
| 17: Dzangal | 178 |
| 18: Vegas, Baby! | 191 |
| 19: On a Wing and a Chook | 206 |
| 20: Kesh Mesh Khan | 222 |
| 21: A Dangerously Close Day | 233 |
| 22: Mark One Eyeball | 244 |

| | |
|---|---|
| 23: Only in Iraq | 263 |
| 24: Human Performance and a Parallel Universe | 278 |
| 25: Welcome to the Jungle | 287 |
| 26: The Rockstar that Wasn't | 306 |
| POSTSCRIPT: 4SQN: The Origins | 315 |
| BACK COVER MATERIAL | 324 |

# FOREWORD

# Murray Turner

It was at the beginning of 2010 when I first met Troy Knight. Troy belonged to a unit that was raised to support 2nd Commando Regiment (2nd Cdo) when conducting Operations in Afghanistan. During all our deployments to the Middle East, we had to have air support, as this support was an integral part of our offensive operations. Having the ability to call in Close Air Support (CAS) was critical to disrupting the enemy, shaping the enemy's behaviour and essentially killing the enemy. Apart from this, also having the ability to relay valuable information to the Insertion and Extraction aircraft, as well as chatting with the UAV operators, was essential.

Special Forces soldiers all have the capability to call in an air strike in extremis, call and direct insert/extract helicopters (helos) and more importantly, have the confidence and knowledge to direct medical extraction assets. These skills are taught to every operator in the unit, but of course, these skills have limitations and regulations. Therefore, having a dedicated JTAC attached to your platoon is an unparalleled luxury that is almost beyond words, because, on top of providing an unparalleled level of offensive air capability, having a dedicated JTAC also frees up an operator to conduct room clearances with his team. Having a CQB/Selection-qualified JTAC has the added advantage of being able to utilise that JTAC for room entries, assist building explosive entry charges and all other aspects of soldiering, if required. Most importantly, it allows him to dedicate his time to planning complex air missions and developing insert and extract plans unhindered.

Meeting Troy for the first time, I could tell that he was an easygoing guy with plenty of experience. He was confident and yet had a relaxed nature that I knew would be important for him to integrate into Delta Company. Delta had spent the whole of 2009 on a domestic counterterrorism (DCT) response and was now building-up to our mid-2010 deployment back to Tarin Kowt for another six-month rotation. We were a fully manned company and our skills were immaculate from being on short notice response for any DCT incidents. During our training over the previous year, we had been tested again and again on every eventuality that could potentially happen on Australian soil, should an incident be a bus, train, aircraft or any other land-based target or any maritime target. In addition, we had navy support from navy clearance divers that were designated to 2nd Commando Troy and the other JTACs were going to join Delta Company, knowing full well that we had just completed an intense, rigorous and very rewarding year honing all our roping, CQB, explosive, night vision and driving skills (amongst many other skills) and to say he needed to hit the ground running was an understatement and Troy didn't disappoint.

Statistically, out of a course of one hundred and thirty candidates that start, forty will make it to the start of the reinforcement courses and of these, twenty-five or so will complete the courses and become badged with the coveted Sherwood Green Beret. A combat controller will complete these gates as well, giving them seamless integration with the men from 2nd Commando Regiment.

Consequently, meeting Troy and introducing him to the platoon, getting him embedded and operational, was a key milestone during early 2010. We had dates for our build-up and consolidation activity, which was in May, based out of Cultana in South Australia. This training and validation activity went off extremely well and when we left, there was a sense of relief and pride that we were expertly set up for a great tour as we had really tested all our 'enablers'. We had an awesome platoon headquarter element including our captain (KR), platoon sergeant (RH) and our attachments like Troy, medic (SB), communications specialist (SW) and others. 'When the shit hits the fan,' as they say, having the ability to apply advanced medical care, call in bombs and communicate with higher, is second to none, and these three guys were the best at it.

We hit the ground running during summer in late June, and it was in the middle of the fighting season. Following a successful handover from Alpha Company indicating key hotspots, Mid and High Value Targets and what remained of Low Value Individuals, we started our planning cycles and started to integrate with our designated air packet that would be assigned to TF66. I was the lead team commander for this rotation and therefore responsible for the ground assault plan for any missions, meaning that I would designate what teams were doing what. This planning would take place with our platoon commander (captain) who would give tactical and operational guidance and objectives finalised through Troy who would communicate and relay mission requirements to our air packet. He was our go-to guy in the team to get helicopters (Black Hawks and Chinooks) and close air support, whether rotary wing or fixed wing (Apaches and/or F-15s, et cetera).

Troy worked hard throughout the planning days to ensure we had every available asset we could get for our missions. He coordinated troop transport, CAS and UAV assets through their different HQ elements and let me tell you synchronising all these into a combat mission is a mind-boggling skill. I'm so glad we had a guy like Troy that could talk the talk and get things done.

# FOREWORD

# Dan Schilling

This is a story of a journey to an unknown destination. That Troy Knight had no idea where the terminus was, or perhaps that there was one at all, is typical of guys who find themselves in the unique force that is Combat Control. Combat Controllers, known universally by the acronym CCT, exist in a state of near invisibility in the public sphere and even across Australia's Defence Force.

There are advantages to such a low organizational profile, as it sometimes affords a freedom of maneuver while deployed to foreign countries and even within a large bureaucracy such as the ADF. The downside comes when lone Combat Controllers show up at a unit they're attached to who have no idea what he is or grasp his diverse skills. Compounding the challenges of integrating into someone else's culture and mission is the guilty by association perception of being an Air Force puke or "Raafie."

Norm's (as we all know Troy here in the States) journey is the parallel evolution of the man and that of Australia's CCT, both of which came at a fortuitous time in Australia's history, joining as they did America's foray into

Afghanistan and Iraq. These battlefields provided opportunities for the SASR and 2 Commando forces to get "wet" in combat after the many decades of no warfare following America's Second Indochina War in Vietnam. The irony for what would become Oz's own CCT was that SAS and 2CDO troopers were used to being supported exclusively by US CCT in Afghanistan and Iraq and were less than enthusiastic about the prospects of an Australian version.

However, back Down Under, wise and prescient members of the RAAF recognized the country's need to have its own force to deliver precision airpower on target or gain entry into contested or denied geography of value to the nation. As often happens in history, when presented with the opportunity to establish something groundbreaking and of great value, those leaders who inevitably rise to the top of peacetime military service saw no need to create what didn't already exist in their understanding of how wars should be fought. You could have asked any Navy leader of the First World War what the value of the airplane would be to combat and without exception the notion would be that it had peripheral value at best if the concept were not dismissed outright.

Never underestimate the ability of a handful of highly motivated and capable humans, however. Norm, along with a few key leaders and fellow NCOs, would not accept the status quo and in the past dozen years built arguably the most versatile force to enter the ADF in a century. This will prove to be of great value in the coming decades of near peer competition with China and the increase in small regional crises within Australia's sphere of influence. For no force can more rapidly introduce military capability into an arena than a Combat Controller. This is perhaps exemplified by the US CCT leading the world's humanitarian response in 2010 when the nation of Haiti literally collapsed and international aid was required within hours to stave off extensive loss of life.

Building and then fielding such a lethal, and simultaneously humanitarian, special operations capability does not happen in a vacuum. The price to the individual as the lone final authority to drop bombs on other humans while performing at a level commensurate with such legendary operators as SASR troopers exacts an unavoidable and extremely high price. Broken marriages, survivor's guilt, alcohol and drug dependencies as coping methods for the former, and the ultimate loss, suicide, are all too common for men in this career. Norm is no exception, as his story attests.

What I can say with some authority is that the very spirit, determination and, as we say here in the States, "true grit" that allow such men to rise to the top of a profession few could ever attempt, let alone master, is that it also provides the very resilience necessary for them to return from combat and killing and somehow find their way back to humanity. I hope that all of them make that journey home.

What is important for you as a reader is to know that such dedicated professionals exist and that should Australia ever face another existential threat like that of the looming Japanese invasion of World War Two (and that so closely aligns The Lucky Country with that of my own homeland to this day) Aussie CCT will be there to deliver death to her enemies, relief to those in need, and rapid response to crises yet to be imagined. On that day Australia's Combat Controllers will be the "First There."

# AUTHOR'S NOTE

## by Brooke Strahan

In all honesty, I've known Troy for less than a year from the time of writing this, however, he is a person that I've felt I've known for years and that's not because I've co-authored his autobiography. Troy and I are very similar in a lot of ways. Like me, he has a strong work ethic, a desire to prove himself (to himself) and can be slightly manipulative and sneaky. Yep, I can definitely be manipulative and sneaky, but I'm probably more conniving and selfish than Troy could ever be. There's also a very good chance that I stole Troy's place at Army recruit training, hence, his being able to tell his story as one of Australia's first RAAF combat controllers.

Troy would do anything for his mates and his children, and you will see this because of the multiple times he has risked his life for others. Troy is an underdog. He looks harmless and unassuming and is often the class clown. In saying this, however, Troy usually wins. Things work out in his favour, even when he has fucked them up. Fuckery is Troy's middle name. He is really good at it. I even suggested giving this book the title, 'FUCKERY: The Troy Knight Story', but for some reason that didn't go down well

At times during the writing of this book, I've come down on Troy harder than a regimental sergeant major. He has put up with my unfiltered feedback, constant demands, crazy suggestions and salty moods. I've been the equivalent to the nagging wife without the benefits.

After reading my two fiction novels, *The Subject* and *The Subject 2: Fade*, Troy contacted me and asked if I would co-author his military autobiography. Troy was honest and humble enough to recognise he needed some assistance in telling his story. I jumped at the opportunity to be part of something bigger than myself.

Troy's story was one that hadn't before been told. There are plenty of Australian Special Forces autobiographies out there, but none that tell the story of the Australian combat controller. I knew it was a very important story to tell, plus Troy had a backstory that also needed to be put into words and more importantly, for himself and his own mental health.

Writing is cathartic. That's one of the main reasons I do it and I encourage others to. The majority of veterans suffer some type of mental health issue and putting pen to paper or fingers to keyboard, allows them to let it out. Writing about the issues that veterans face opens up the conversation around mental health that is so prevalent in ex-serviceman and none more so than those involved in the Special Forces and elite combat roles.

For me, this was such an important part of Troy's story. His personal mental health and the toll his job has had on it needed to be spoken about. It was important to me for a partly selfish reason. Through the telling of Troy's story, it helped me further my own understanding of where a Special Forces soldier's head is at, following time in combat. I say this because two of my greatest loves were both Australian commandos. Both stole my heart and then broke it. I understand this was not done intentionally, but it has taken me actually getting inside Troy's head, someone who has been there and done that for me to get some of my own personal closure, so many years later.

Though Troy is no longer serving, he goes to war every day, battling the demons that try to break him but as he has shown, time and time again, he is strong and courageous and will not be broken by anything or anyone.

# AUTHOR'S NOTE

## by Troy Knight

Everyone who knows me can vouch for my ability to tell a story at an event, party or a bar. The idea to write a book was never mine. It was suggested on several occasions to me, as I have had an eventful life and people enjoyed hearing about the stupid shit I did. I made people laugh with my true-life stories. Seeing people smile as I told them about the time I landed in a chook pen from the sky, I realised it was joyful to give joy to others. If it were the medieval times, I may well have been considered the court jester or in my own eyes, the village idiot.

The idea of writing *Havoc-06* started to gain momentum inside me and I grew in confidence the more seriously I took it. *Havoc-06* was my call sign. After passing two years of training, I was awarded a coveted beret and the wings of an Australian combat controller. I was the sixth one to do so, hence the call sign, *Havoc-06*.

I began to jot down notes on possible anecdotes and I started to openly chat to combat controllers and operators from my 2nd Commando Regiment about the writing journey I was starting to embark upon.

Telling the guys I used to work with that I was going to be writing a military autobiography was not easy. We are brought up to be in the shadows and as the silent professionals, when we are no longer in this fighting role, I think it is important to tell the stories and professionalism of these men. In comparison to the US Navy SEALs or Australia's own Special Air Service Regiment, combat control is a relatively new capability and much like 2nd Commando Regiment, it has been left in the background with the stories of their exploits.

I never intended to write the book as a 100 per cent warfighting, Wild West gunslinging type of story. I wanted to capture the Australia larrikinism, the camaraderie, the emotions and the struggles that go into working and deploying within the Australian Defence Force.

Upon leaving the Defence Force, I finally decided to write the book and actually committed to it. There was a problem though, I had no idea how things worked in the publishing industry. One person changed that for me and began the ball rolling, that person being JJ Hackett. Using his connections, JJ reached out to people and within days, I had phone calls from the likes of published military authors such as Mark Donaldson VC, Matt Hall (former F-18 pilot and Red Bull Air Racer) and another former F-18 pilot who goes by the pseudonym Mac 'Serge' Tucker. Along with this, I had interviews with some of Australia's leading publishing houses encouraging me to pitch them a synopsis. With JJ's help the synopsis was written and pitched.

I was lucky enough to be picked by a very reputable and well-known publishing house. Again, sometimes in this life, it is who you know not what you know. As I began to put words to paper, it became apparent that I needed significant help with my writing. JJ was busy and so the search began.

It was like the clouds parted and this ray of shining light beamed through. Enter Brooke Strahan. I first met Brooke through the power of social media. She had illustrated a piece of artwork for a friend and the unique style of the piece captured my attention.

I messaged her and sent her a few pictures I wanted her to illustrate for me. Realising she was already a published author and always looking to expand my knowledge, I may have accidently (deliberately) let slip that I was writing an autobiography.

'Oh, I have a few books, fictional ones, published. I'll flick you through some e-copies for a gander,' came her response.

As our friendship grew and after reading her two books, *The Subject* and *The Subject 2: Fade*, I could easily see the passion she had for not only her illustrations but for her writing. Not being a massive fiction fan myself, I read her books for research. I wanted my story to be explained correctly. The thing about Brooke was that she understood. She got me. I discovered the types of things she did in her spare time, such as helping and supporting not-for-profit organisations and promoting positivity and an outdoor lifestyle.

As I read her fiction series, I was enthralled by the way she explained her two lead characters. It was like I was there sharing the journey. She made her characters come to life and they captivated me. The critics always say when watching a movie, if you become the character or become a part of the movie, then it has achieved its purpose. The same thing happened when I read her books.

After meeting with Brooke and her amazing husband, the choice was simple. Brooke keeps true to herself, which is an outstanding quality, because not only does she have a background in the Defence Force, but also with security, other government agencies and is a professional writer. I asked her if she would be interested in co-authoring my book and Brooke responded with her usual big smile and with an even bigger, 'Yes!'

Brooke and I talk or FaceTime most days, bouncing ideas off each other. Again, I thank her husband for his patience because I am often like an emotionally needy child. I tend to have this need for guidance and would find myself thinking, 'Is there anything this woman cannot do?' We all know that one kid growing up that excelled at everything, but in my case, that kid is a six-foot, blonde woman.

Brooke has been my muse throughout this journey, inspiring my writing, pushing me to deadlines and educating me, which has decidedly improved my writing. Hell, I even proofread my work these days, well, sometimes.

Brooke, words cannot thank you enough.

# To my children

One early morning, after training the previous night, I was suddenly awoken by a work colleague. Still groggy from lack of sleep, I heard him telling me to turn on the television.

I switched on the box to be confronted by the vision of one of the New York's Twin Towers on fire and watched as a commercial airliner flew into the second tower. At the point, I didn't realise how that moment would influence my life.

This life-changing event saw me deploy for the better part of two decades and as a result, suffer from not bonding with my children and also failed relationships because of my job. When I was not deployed, I was training to be deployed. I was always training for that next contingency, training to push and develop a new defence capability.

'To my children, I am sorry for all you have endured and suffered, but now I look forward to our future.

I write this book for you as much as for myself.

# To my fallen mates

Your stories will always be told. Never forgotten.

To the operators of Delta and Bravo Commando Company groups that I did my special operation task group rotations within Afghan and Iraq, I thank you for the good times and the seamless integration and acceptance. I don't care what the Army policy is on death symbols, you guys will always be the Punishers and Convicts to me.

To my fellow combat controllers who made everything possible,

I thank you. Keep fighting the good fight.

And most of all, to the men and women of 4SQN.

Keep pushing the limits.

# INTRODUCTION

# Norm, Norm, but Different

'Cleared hot,' I transmitted.

'One away,' was the calm reply in my headset.

'You, beauty,' I thought, 'my first release.'

Still, I was shitting myself, hoping like all hell that I had provided the correct data to the aircrew because with a GPS bomb, once it's off the rails, you've bought it, and nothing could stop its now inexorable flight to its destination. As I sat there waiting for the *swack*, I wondered how I had ever come to be in this position

My name is Troy. My mates know me as Norm, TK and if they want to wind me up, The North-Innisfail Champ. I was born in Brisbane, Queensland in 1977 to a single mother Shirley Knight. My biological father disappeared when he found out Mum was pregnant. I never knew his name. Luckily for me, Mum met a lovely young man who accepted the package deal. Terry is the only man I've ever known as Dad, and he and Mum went on to give me a brother and a sister.

I grew up your typical Queensland boy, surfing, playing rugby league and generally looking for mischief. In primary school, I was a near straight-A student and the captain of a few sporting teams. During my teen years, I started to take a downhill slide. If you asked them, my parents would tell you I went a little wild. I ditched school, discovered alcohol, got into fights, drove fast cars and found women. There may even have been the odd run-in with the Queensland Police. The boys I knocked around with then are now fathers too, but when we sit around a fire and look back on it, we wouldn't change a thing.

Even at a young age I enjoyed having a laugh.

The boundary-pushing and risk-taking fuelled my thirst for adventure and it is that part of my nature that saw me subsequently travel to Afghanistan, Iraq and beyond, all at the behest of the Australian Government.

Mum and Dad worked long hours to pay for our sport and to make ends meet, so I naturally spent a lot of my time with my grandparents. From a young age, both my grandfathers played a major role in shaping the man I was to become. Mervin the hard-as-nails boxer from the Jimmy Sharman circuit, who later worked for the railways, inspired me with his firm work ethic and tenacity, in the face of adversity. Mervin the bushman taught me to shoot. He and his brothers were crack shots and would often tell me so. My first handling of a rifle would see me shaking and shedding a tear or two. I had been on a few shooting trips with him but was never allowed to shoot. This was about to change. Calling me over, he said, 'It is time, Troy, time we teach you to shoot.' He handed me a .22-calibre semiautomatic rifle. It was just after my tenth birthday.

I was keen as mustard or so I thought. Once I had the rifle in my hands, I started to tremble. To this day, I don't know why. I was overcome with emotion and began to cry.

Pop did not understand. 'What is wrong, Troy? You have been pestering me to shoot and now you are crying about it,' he gruffly said. 'Just aim it like I showed you and pull the trigger,' he proclaimed.

I finally summoned up enough courage and pulled the trigger. I am not even sure that I aimed. After that initial shot, I grew in confidence and began emptying the 10-round magazine into the tree which served as a target. Towards the end of the magazine, I even hit the tree a couple of times. I finished the magazine, unloaded and reloaded with another. I was growing in confidence. I had wiped the tears away and now I had my big boy pants on. The second magazine went a lot smoother than the first and from memory, I hit the target with every shot. Pity that mantra did not follow me to Afghanistan. I may have hit a few more bad guys.

Dave, my other grandfather, was a carpenter who had fought in New Guinea during World War II and would regale me with stories of battle and fighting the Japanese. My bedtime stories were about him fighting the Japanese in the jungles of Papua New Guinea. Even from that early age, I remember him talking about how crafty, cunning and ruthless the Japanese Imperial Forces were. To me, it was all a wild adventure and where my early childhood fantasy of military life began. When Dave passed away, I was given all of his personal military trinkets and his small yet valuable collection of Japanese war treasure. Both grandfathers, without realising it, lit the fire that led me unerringly to the military.

\*\*\*

In September 1999, having just completed my butcher's apprenticeship, the East Timor crisis kicked off. With excitement at the thought of going to war, I rushed to the Australian Defence Force recruiting office in Townsville. I scored quite well in the many tests and was offered several jobs, including the one I coveted as an army rifleman. Unfortunately, army recruit training was bottlenecked for eight months and that was just too long for me to wait. Dismayed and nearly out the door, I was stopped by an Air Force sergeant who asked me if I knew about the Airfield Defence Guards. I did not, but when he said I could start in February and that the ADGies were already deployed to Timor, I seized the opportunity and jumped in, boots and all.

Ironically, by the time I graduated from basic training and started my first posting at the RAAF base at Amberley, the unit had already redeployed home, while the Army infantry battalions kept up their rotations for many years to come. Disappointed but undeterred, I applied myself to my new trade, hoping I would eventually get my chance at my dream, combat operations.

# 1

# A Dirty RAAFie

After ten weeks of being treated like a kid during Air Force recruit training, I was now enjoying being treated a little more like an adult. The previous 10 weeks at the RAAF base at Edinburgh could not have gone quick enough, but now at Amberley, I had begun my initial employment training for my RAAF mustering in the airfield defence guard (ADG).

The ADG basic course was certainly a change of pace compared to the recruit training. There was physical training (PT) in the morning and most afternoons and a lot more time out bush, which I enjoyed. There were, however, theory lessons in which I struggled to stay awake, often finding myself staring out into space, thinking about how long it had been since I had seen my beautiful wife.

Having passed out of basic training, I was afforded luxuries, such as time off base and at least one day off on weekends, however, it was not all beer and skittles and I was about to get a big taste of things to come.

Our first big challenge came in the form of a food and sleep-deprivation weekend. This alleged downtime involved carrying heavy things, pushing transport that should have been towed or driven and digging defensive pits throughout the night. While digging, I deliberated on how I should have been getting my much-needed beauty sleep.

'Get on the bus if you want!' shouted the instructors. They continued, 'It is comfortable and heated.' I watched throughout the weekend as the broken and weak climbed on the bus. 'Stuffed if I'm getting on that bus,' I thought myself, adjusting my pack for the millionth time. I was far from leading the group, but I wasn't giving up now, I had already come too far to let weakness win.

Weakness didn't win and I managed to push through the activity and not get on the coach that was following us around. For me, this activity opened my eyes to what resilience, toughness and fortitude is and how they are similar but very different traits that one needs to develop. This activity also set the standard for my military career that every training activity always ended with me doing something stupid.

***

A number of weeks had been spent teaching and honing our skills in the field. A big stand out for me, was learning fire and movement. Fire and movement are the basis of keeping yourself alive, while getting shot at. In theory, it would allow one to survive a contact but as I later found out in life, it is purely the geometry of chance. Sometimes you survive and sometimes you do not.

Initially, I enjoyed throwing myself onto hard ground, a requirement of fire and movement. Now, the sands of time have changed and my body, like so many other veterans, is swearing at me for it.

The field training exercises, which had been built purely around this fire and movement skill, had come to an end. It was at this time when those on the course were introduced to, let's call it, an end-of-month base drinks and raffles night. This night was run by the mess and quite often raised much-needed money for charity or local organisations.

After cleaning weapons and equipment, we were given the standard what is and what is not brief by our instructors. Part of this brief pertained to the no-go zone for us surrounding the on-base entertainment. 'What the?' I thought when we were informed not to attend the fundraiser. 'Ah well, so be it,' I said to myself.

So it should have been, but I decided to attend the evening affair, dragging a few of my mates along with me. A few hours into the night, we were all having a good time. We had managed to hide in the crowd avoiding detection. That was until we were spotted by two of our instructors.

'Now what were you told, lads?' came a slightly inebriated voice from behind us. I jumped up and froze. Luckily, one of the boys replied before I could get in with my usual smart-arse comment. Unfortunately, his reply to the instructor wasn't much better than mine would have been.

There ensued a few choices words from our party-pooping friends. 'Get the fuck out,' was one of the less offensive phrases that I remember. Before we could leave, it somehow nearly escalated into fisticuffs. Naturally, by this stage, I was like, 'Stuff it, I'm all in here.' In all fairness, I had caused the whole thing.

We must have made quite the spectacle because the crowd of onlookers grew. A few of them came over and defused the situation. With the situation defused, we did as ordered and returned to our lines.

Angry and alcohol effected, I announced to the boys, 'Stuff this, I am going back!'

'No, you are not, Knighty,' my more sensible mates retorted.

I didn't listen and started to walk away when *bam,* I was crash tackled to the ground! One of the guys was a gun rugby player and had put me straight to the ground with one of the best hits I have ever had, on or off the field. While getting held down, it was decided that the best way to restrain me was to hogtie my hands and feet with zip ties.

'Just great,' I thought, as everyone came out to observe the ruckus that was me being detained for my own good. The onlookers seemed to take great pleasure in watching it all.

Despite this, I was and still am impressed by my level of mobility to have both my hands and feet trussed behind my back.

The following week rolled around and naturally the squadron warrant officer had heard about our shenanigans and we were hauled into the boss's office.

'You are all very lucky to be remaining in the course,' the boss informed us, after giving us a good dressing down.

I stood there, trying to look serious and sorry, thinking how maybe I should try not to look for mischief and obey a simple order for once. Then, the interrogation began with the boss asking who the instructors were? I played dumb and so did the others. None of us were about to rat out the guys who taught us and had our respect. I mean, you don't shit in your own backyard.

Realising they were not going to get the required information from us, the bosses gave up. We got sent on our way with the warning, 'Keep your heads down and out of trouble.'

'Good work, lads,' my section commander said, pulling us troublemakers aside. He had a wry smirk on his face as he continued, 'You kept your mouth shut. That goes a long way with trust.'

Surprisingly, I did pull my head in for the rest of the course and managed to graduate unscathed, with my grandfather Dave there to watch my graduation parade. I was very proud and chuffed to have the World War II veteran on my support team.

After the graduation parade, my grandfather congratulated me, shaking my hand. He leant in and said, 'I'm proud of you Troy, but you are still a dirty RAAFie.'

***

The whole reason I had joined the Royal Australian Air Force and gone into the ADG mustering was to be deployed to Timor. Upon graduating, I was given our squadron posting and I was posted to 2 Airfield Defence Squadron (2AFDS). It was at this same time, I received news that the squadron would be returning from East Timor and not be replaced.

'Arrggh,' I screamed out loud. I was gutted. It was like my whole purpose in life had just been thrown out the window. 'I've just gone through all that training crap to walk around base and look at aircraft,' I thought to myself, shattered.

Life continued on and I tried to find purpose in other activities. The disappointment of missing out on the deployment would be one I would become familiar with, as it would not be the first nor last deployment that I missed out on. I have lost track of how many deployments I have been 'stood to' at short notice to move sitting at air movements.

***

After a short bus ride, we arrived at Greenbank training area for the start of my arrivals course. This course was the conversion course into squadron tactics, techniques and procedures. We were ushered into World War II-style huts as the lead instructor informed us in a cool, calm voice, instead of the usual yelling I had become accustomed to, where to place our gear and next timings. 'This is a pleasant change,' I thought, 'being treated like an adult.'

The pleasant change, however, was short-lived. Jube was the nickname for us new guys or inexperienced airmen. Due to failing to follow a simple instruction, another Jube (not me for once) turned, what I thought was going to be Camp Holiday, into a fucking royal suckfest. I should have had more foresight because, in reality, it was always going to happen.

During the five days at Suckfest 2000, we were introduced to patrol-level tactics as opposed to section level. An ADG patrol comprised of four to six people. A half-section if you will. There was constant shooting from all ranges and a variety of weapons. The beauty of an Airfield Defence Squadron is that, for a week, we had the allocation of ammunition equivalent to the amount an infantry battalion had in a month but only a quarter of the people to use it. There were multiple navigation exercises and a lot of physical shit. The instructors seemed to enjoy these the most.

After being in the squadron for a couple of months, I started hearing rumours about the Jube Olympics. 'It must be another preselection course,' I thought. But to my surprise, this was something different. It was something actually fun and purely for humour. For once, no one was being made to do anything they did not want to do.

As part of military training, we do a run dodge jump (RDJ). It's a military-orientated obstacle course and the Jube Olympics had us competing in this RDJ but with a twist. The twist was that every obstacle had a challenge (apart from the challenge of the actual obstacles). The challenge came in the form of dry Weet-Bix, warm beer and various other concoctions that not even Harry Potter could conjure up.

Needless to say, I made it to the finish and I felt terrible for days after. The witches' potions had indeed worked their magic. At what I thought was the end of the Jube Olympics, it was announced that there was one activity left for us Jubes to survive, in order for us to be successfully initiated. This activity was Jube boxing. In the upcoming weeks, we were to square off against each other for the sole amusement of the squadron.

If there was a grudge match or someone you wanted to square up against, you were free to organise it, 'Place your names on the board,' we were told.

I got along with most people, so I had no one who I particularly wanted to beat the shit out of (or at least try) so I just got paired up with someone. This someone was a heavy-set guy who talked himself up constantly and underperformed. Let's call him Fish Fingers.

As the weeks went by, so did the Jube boxing matches until it was finally my time to mill. I say mill because most of the guys had no boxing experience and used to just punch on.

I had no real plan going into my fight. I just wanted to knock him down or out. Most of us on the course had disliked him for his constant shit stories, lies and laziness. The referee signalled to fight and there was no bell.

The round started slow as I was just jabbing my way in and moving around, looking like I knew what I was doing. *Swack* suddenly came the sound of Fish Fingers' haymaker that clocked me fair in the temple. The hit buckled me and I saw stars. With my heart rate going up, I struggled not to panic as more punches rained down my way.

I managed to move. Okay, I ran. I ran away to the other side of the ring to regain my composure. Luckily for me, the referee signalled the end of the round. 'Thank you, baby Jesus,' I thought.

Funny story about my corner man. He could box. He had knocked out three guys in one afternoon of Jube boxing and was subsequently banned from partaking in it again. He had played at the top level of rugby league in the country and went on to serve in another Special Forces unit. He was an all-round top guy and he was now in my corner giving me hot tips for round two.

It was nearing the end of round two when I caught my opponent with a body rip. My hit must have done some damage as he crumbled onto his side and winced. Sensing something was up and with little to no fight IQ, I went in and rained punches down on my old mate Fish Fingers.

It was not pretty but it worked. The referee jumped in and stopped the fight, declaring me the winner. I wasn't exactly proud as, in all honesty, I had just been lucky. Sore and spent, I was glad the whole thing was over.

***

It was Autumn 2004 and we had been humping heavy weights around Canungra training area for a couple of days. 'I was back, baby!' Back at Canungra for the illustrious military skills competition that the combined recon/sniper team, I had been part of, had won only the previous year! I was, however, not back in quite the same capacity.

I had been given the distinguished opportunity to be the section commander for my combined team. I use the word distinguished, well, facetiously. I did not want to be their leader. While I had no problem with motivating people to perform their roles, I severely lacked experience in leadership, and I had avoided doing the section commander course as though it were the plague.

So, I avoided my section leader course because that would see me get promoted and moved out of recon/snipers into the rifle flights. Recon/snipers was where it was at and I was determined not to move on.

My team this year was most certainly combined. There were a couple of us recon and sniper types, but I had some assault pioneers, a clerk and a couple of guys who were semibusted.

As this military skills competition progressed, it went the way you might expect. The weak fell away and my leadership tactics (or lack thereof) absolutely sucked.

Though this year's competition was nowhere near as physically exhausting as the previous year, in the early morning of day four, it become apparent that one of the guys was carrying an injury. I spoke to him and he reassured me he could go on. He was a recon guy, so I do not know if it was my stern words that kept him pushing or his own willpower. That was something that I would find out later.

My team kept pushing hard through into the night, before finding our bed-down location for the evening. It was a non-tactical rest, meaning we did not have to rotate someone on piquet or a guard.

Not long after dozing off, I was abruptly awoken by a deep, dull moaning. 'What the hell is that?' I asked myself. As we all were closely situated, I sat up to investigate the noise.

'Who is that?' I asked in a grumpy tone, unhappy to have been woken from my precious beauty sleep.

'Knighty, it is OB.' OB was the recon guy who had pushed on with his injury from the morning. He was, I discovered later, in some pain.

'What is it, OB?' I asked, not overly concerned.

'I'm fucked, mate, my stomach is killing me,' OB claimed, clutching his mid-section.

Being the great leader I was, I retorted, 'Shut up and get some sleep, mate, you will be right.'

After dozing off, I was alerted again to OB's dull yet eerie moans.

'OB, what is up?' I asked again, not impressed at being woken once again.

'It is getting worse,' OB could barely stammer.

'JB,' I shouted at my 2IC, 'Go check him out.' JB did as instructed as I rolled over onto my side and closed my eyes.

JB was similar to myself and did not want to be promoted. He wanted to stay in recon his whole life. But like myself, we both got volunteered for the duties of section commander and second in charge.

After attending to OB, JB returned to my side and spoke, 'Knighty, yeah mate, this isn't too good. There's something seriously wrong.'

I radioed through to the command post and they immediately medevaced OB out and to the hospital. It turned out that OB had a hernia and had carried all that equipment with it. No wonder the bloke had been in so much pain!

My team finished the military skills competition with less than half our combined section and placed third. Separating first place from third place was only a matter of three points. Though we lost, I was happy to place third behind two seasoned section commanders with their dedicated sections.

I was not happy with my leadership. I had failed OB. I had seriously lacked empathy in the pursuit of winning. A lot of people will say, 'Mission, men, self.' That is true, but it is circumstantial. This event was just a military skills competition, for God's sake, and I did not take the health and welfare of my men seriously. Leadership-wise, I did learn a lot from that activity. For me, I was just lucky OB was a hard dude or I could have injured an outstanding airman for nothing. Big lesson learnt.

***

A lot of people ask me if I regret joining the RAAF ADG mustering, rather than Army infantry. My answer, 'Never.'

I had three deployments and attended multiple courses that I would not have had the opportunity to do in the infantry battalion. I have made mates that I am still close with after twenty plus years and several of them have let me be their groomsman. One can never regret such close bonds of mateship and camaraderie. We may have just been dirty RAAFies, but we were good ones.

Live fire pairs with H&K MP5

Recon early 00's

# 2

# Lantana

I never wanted out of the recon and sniper flight. Early in my career I had decided to go down the reconnaissance and, eventually, the sniper route. Recon and snipers. Sounds cool, doesn't it? I mean, that's the type of guy that every other guy wants to be and every girl wants to date. Or so I thought.

I had already had a crack at a 6RAR-run sniper course earlier in the year and failed miserably. Apparently, it turned out that I have buttons for eyes and could barely see any of the military items placed out in the bush. At the time I was devastated, because there's nothing cooler than being a rockstar sniper, but now I can laugh and say, 'Should have gone to Specsavers.'

The basic sniper course had multiple components to it. Contrary to popular belief, there is a lot more to it than just shooting a rifle. The test I failed was the static observation lane. This particular test is conducted by laying on the ground with binoculars and a spotting scope. You have a time limit placed on you which adds extra pressure. I had to lay down and sketch the surrounding area. The idea is to commence finding military items amongst these surrounds. This was the time that I not only found out that my eyesight was up shit creek, but so was my artistic talent. I sucked at sketching. 'Knight, I've seen better sketches completed by my four year old,' one of the instructors informed me. 'Great,' I thought, 'Now I'll never be one of those soldiers turned artist.' This sudden realisation that I was completely lacking in sketching ability added more pressure and, needless to say, I had failed my observation.

If my memory serves me correctly, you have about eight practice attempts before going into the badge test. I'm fairly sure I failed all of them. This was definitely a highlight of my career, for all the wrong reasons. I remember feeling so pissed off and frustrated at myself for failing. For a long time after this, I continually questioned myself, 'What was I doing wrong? Why could I not see the items in the bush? Had I applied all the techniques I was taught? If I was scanning the bush using the correct methodology than why had this failed me?' I had failed, hence, I was a failure. When you have already reached such a level in your career, it's hard to just let something like this go. I would say it is built into the military rockstar DNA or maybe, I was just being too hard on myself.

***

Six months and some extra training later, I was given a second crack at the sniper course.

This particular course was a joint 2AFDS and 6RAR course. Located in sunny Queensland, it was being run out of the Wide Bay training area, located just north of beautiful Noosa on the Sunshine Coast.

Excited, everybody on the course trotted down to the Q-Store to start the rigmarole of signing-out all the logistical items required. The excitement quickly turned to the mundane, as the rest of the morning was used to sign-out our rifles, ammunition and get the required orders. One of the sets of orders read out was the convoy orders. These convoy orders were the most convoluted piece of dribble I had ever heard. Word of advice, if you ever have trouble sleeping at night, then get your hands on a set of convoy orders and read them. Much better than any sleeping pill.

The sniper course is a massive undertaking, as are most courses in the military. On the course is not just the wannabe snipers like myself. There are more support personnel than snipers. Of course, there are the instructors, but there's also the cooks, logistics staff, administration staff and signal operators or as I like to call them, radio nerds.

One of the radio nerds was named Matt. He was a good mate of mine, and we had completed recruit training and our ADG basic course together. He was an ADG, but he went onto specialise in radios. Because of his last name being Martin, he was known as Marty. Original, I know.

As part of those boring convoy orders, you are allocated a seat on the vehicles. I copped a shit seat on this six-wheeled hunk of crap. This type of thing was a common occurrence for me as I liked to gob off a fair bit, being a smart-arse or a little cheeky as I prefer to call it. The six-wheeled hunk of crap that I refer to is an off-road vehicle made by Land Rover. In all fairness, this vehicle is hardy and has a role to play, however, when riding in one of these contraptions, you are sitting sideways in the back of it and exposed to the wind. The whole thing sucks arse.

Depending on who you talk to, the other vehicle, a Land Rover 110, was a better deal. My mate Marty had gotten this better deal being placed in the non-sucky Land Rover 110. Marty was the type of guy who would give you the shirt off his back. Me, on the other hand, I am not that type of guy. I'm the type that will keep my own shirt and try to take yours, so I don't freeze to death. With Marty being so nice and me not so nice, I thought I might be able to take advantage of this. I tried to do a deal with Marty to swap seats. 'C'mon, mate,' I said, 'If you take my seat, I will buy you a box of Mars Bars.' Marty, who usually loved junk food, wasn't being quite as nice as usual and wouldn't have a bar of it. 'Nope,' he replied with a smirk on his face. I heard the convoy drivers start up their engines, so I decided to give up and take my assigned seat in the piece of crap that was my ride.

'Fuck! The Land Rover 110 has gone off the road!' one of the lads yelled. This sentence immediately woke me up from my sleep caused by the convoy orders. The convoy stopped immediately. We jumped out of the shitbucket, running back towards the Land Rover 110. As we approached, we could see the vehicle had gone off a five-metre embankment and into some very thick lantana. While running, I remember joking with the lads about shit driving. I was very naïve about the brutality of cars.

I was first or second to reach the vehicle and what I saw I can't unsee. The scene was utter carnage. The vehicle had torn into two pieces. We found the cook first and he was severed in two. His body was completely separated from the waist up. The sight of the dismembered body immediately put me into a state of shock. I can only describe this feeling as like being in a dream. Everything became foggy and I started walking around in a daze, any training going out the window. I was suddenly grabbed by one of the 6RAR snipers who talked me back to my senses and into the reality of the situation in front of me. The sniper and I went looking for Marty. We found Marty, he was motionless and we began to assess his injuries. Marty was non-responsive. 'Fuck it,' I thought to myself. As we took further assessment of the situation, we saw that Marty's neck was almost completely severed. Marty was dead.

Still in shock but doing what I knew needed to be done, I helped clean up the area as much as I could and cover the bodies of the deceased. As advised, we moved back to the top of the road and waited for the emergency services to arrive.

I wanted to cry, but I would not let it out in front of my mates. I should have, it's what was needed, but I didn't cry. No one cried. It's funny, the military teaches you to look after your mates but not how to look after yourself. Maybe that's just human nature? We, as individuals, always seem to emotionally look after our friends before we look after ourselves. Zero self-care.

The emergency services arrived, surveyed and assessed the crash site. It took some time for the members to retrieve the bodies. The radio batteries were causing a safety hazard. Due to the accident, the batteries had begun to leak gas. Most military batteries contain lithium gas, and that gas is carcinogenic. The gas was present when I had run initially to the crash site, so who knows if I might end up with cancer down the track?

Because of the hazardous material, we had to wait for the specialist chemicals team from the Queensland Fire Service to arrive. The CO of our unit was advised and the order was given for the majority of guys to return to base where the CO had recalled the unit to tell them the news. Problem was, none of us wanted to leave our mates behind. Arguments that nearly lead to fisticuffs started to happen. I realise now, that this was just part of our grief, and the anger primarily covered our sadness. A good mate of mine Schulzy stepped in and stated he would stay, with one other person. The one other person was not me. We were told not to mention this to anyone, as the families of the deceased were yet to be informed of the tragic news. We all nodded in agreement to this order and, as we mounted the truck, we turned our phones off.

The drive back to base was a sombre one. I was numbed and emotionless. I did not feel like talking and all I wanted was to get back to see my own beautiful children. It had dawned on me that if I had swapped seats with Marty, that could have been me. If I had been more persuasive with my bargaining and if Marty had been more of his usual selfless self, it would have been me that would be dead. But I wasn't dead and I had a million questions in my head. My head banged with 'what ifs' and my heart raced. It took me a few days to shake the headbanging and heart palpitations. I knew that you couldn't dwell on the 'what ifs' in life and those sliding door moments.

On arrival to the unit, I was greeted by my family. My then wife was friends with Marty's wife, so she had already heard the tragic news. The unit had recalled the whole squadron and the boys were told to have their families with them. A support team was brought in, consisting of a chaplain, psychologist and various others to assist in grief counselling. Us guys from the crash site were whisked off to receive counselling straight away. This angered me for some reason. I didn't want to talk to some stranger about my feelings. All I wanted was to be surrounded by my family and my mates from the unit. Protocol is, however, protocol and so I was made to try to talk.

I understand it was a hard job for the counsellors, as none of us wanted to talk to anyone or share our emotions. It was definitely a brief meeting for us in there. After this initial counselling session, we joined the rest of our mates where we were exposed to some more counselling group sessions and told the usual, 'We are here to talk if needed and this is what we offer.' The chaplain did his thing with a quick speech which was more like a sermon. 'Fuck me,' I thought. Religion was the last thing I needed and or wanted. 'What I need and want is a drink.' Well, if there is a God, he heard me because they opened the boozer and we were allowed a beer for an early send-off. The irony of this was that Marty didn't even drink.

I only drank half my beer and I remember thinking, 'There had to be a first for everything.' The reality was that I just wanted to get home and spend time with my family.

Yet when I got home, I knew I was angry and unsettled. I spoke to my wife about what I had seen and my actions at the crash site. She tried her best to understand and support me, but I was still struggling with my emotions or lack thereof. I had really felt helpless at the site and I kept remembering how I froze in the moment. 'Fuck you, Troy,' I thought to myself. 'You want combat and you can't even operate at a crash site. How are you going to act on operations?' The voice of my inner critic had become loud and clear, slowly nibbling away at my self-confidence and sense of self.

I had never seen anything like that before. It wasn't the first time I'd had friends die on me. Growing up, Tim was my best mate and I had lost him to cancer. Fuck cancer! I had cried and sobbed for days over him, allowing myself to naturally grieve, but for some reason, I would not let myself grieve now. The military was already starting to change me. The camaraderie of the lads and heroic nature of the job would not let me. This was the first of many testing moments in the camos and it would surely not be the last.

Marty's send-off was legendary. The wake was a big event, and they even named the bar after him which again was ironic because, as I mentioned, he was a non-drinker. I'm not sure if the bar is still named after him? I hope it is.

Following the accident, The Queensland police carried out their investigations and I believe the RAAF police carried out theirs. We were all interviewed. The inquests came back inconclusive. There was a lack of sufficient evidence to know exactly why the vehicle had swerved from the road. Did the driver fall asleep? Was there something it had to swerve for, such as an object or an animal on the road maybe? The Land Rover 110 was fitted and decked out with a mobile telecommunications hub and was known to be notoriously heavy. A military convoy's speed is, however, limited. To this day, Marty's family and I don't know the cause of the accident.

The sniper course got canned. None of us were keen to attend after the tragic event. This gave me a break and some much-needed extra time to face my nemesis, the static observation activity.

It's funny how certain things can trigger particular memories. Unsurprisingly, writing about Marty triggers many fond memories of him and the time we spent together, but the smell of lantana triggers my memories too. One memory is of a hot day in the Ipswich summer when we were conducting fire and movement attacks. Fire and movement is the way the military ground force assaults an enemy objective. It's hard work on its own, without adding in the environmental factors. You basically throw yourself to the ground and crawl around, shoot, get back to your feet, run towards the enemy and repeat. It is not a fun activity. I will be honest, it is probably the reason I joined combat control, because I got to swan around in four-star hotels with aircrew.

This particular hot Ipswich day was not a good one for Marty. He had the machine gun. A heavier weapon that can basically shoot a shit ton more bullets at a higher rapid-fire rate than a rifle. It is an absolute pig of a thing to operate. Oh my God, the look on Marty's face. My friend was not known for his superior fitness, that's for sure. Mid contact, I burst out laughing at how much he was obviously hurting. See, I told you I wasn't always that nice a person. I was not the only one berating him though. He had a course instructor making his life harder than it already was. Suddenly, it was my turn to get hammered by the course instructor, as his attention had turned to me following my outburst. Just another instance of where my mouth got me into trouble. After knocking off but still smelling of sweat, dirt and lantana, Marty said to me, 'Thanks, mate.' I looked at him and asked, 'What for?'

'For getting the instructor off my arse,' Marty replied.

We both laughed together.

# 3

# Nitro Circus, Iraq

A military skills competition? Doesn't sound that hard. Sounds more like a chance for a bunch of blokes to run around showing off how good they are? Well, you can fuck that idea right off.

The military skills competition was the most physically and mentally gruelling activity I had undertaken in my life, up to that point. The competition was conducted at the notorious Canungra training area, only thirty minutes inland from the beautiful Gold Coast. Though the beaches, night clubs and bikini-clad meter maids were within arm's reach, they might as well have been a million miles away.

Canungra is fabled in the ADF for its treacherous jungle-cloaked mountains, poisonous snakes, enormous spiders and for being the hunting ground of the most daunting of predators, the warrant officer class one.

For the competition, I was part of a five-man combined reconnaissance/sniper team. We had humped heavy shit for five long hot days, all while dodging snakes, with minimal food and next to no sleep. It was a struggle to remember, let alone, perform basic military field skills.

After living out the hashtag #thestruggleisreal, the competition was done and so were we.

Exhausted, we waited for the results. Despite the fact we were spent, we still displayed the usual recon/sniper cockiness, spilling over into hubris and we were certain we had nailed it or at least 'pulled a Bradbury'.

When our team was awarded first place, we were understandably stoked and ready to celebrate our win along with the Gold Coast's finest, however the Commanding Officer had other plans for us.

Winner winner chicken dinner. Recon sniper team that won military skills 2003.

'Hurry up, get changed, clean your weapons and get back to base,' the CO ordered, immediately after congratulating us on our win. 'What the...?' We collectively responded.

The CO cut us short, saying we would be briefed upon our return to base. Well, I'm sure you can imagine the conversation that ensued between the boys during that 90-minute drive back to the base and the words Iraq and Deployment were going back and forth like a tennis ball.

It was 2003 and we had all been following the Iraq War on the news, however, the only ADF personnel getting a crack at it were the jets and Special Forces guys. Imagine my surprise, when during the brief on base, I was told I would be deploying to Iraq. I personally thought I had won an all-expenses-paid trip to the Whitsundays. 'Yeah, baby it's on!' I convinced myself.

\*\*\*

Landing at Baghdad International Airport, I was still on a high, despite the logistics of getting there. I truly was convinced I had won the military version of the lottery. It was just after ANZAC Day and not long after the US Army's 3rd Infantry Division had wiped out all resistance. There was no time to settle in, instead we got to work straight away.

The first there, US combat controllers (many of whom are still my friends), relinquished control of the airfield to our RAAF air traffic controllers, so there was definitely no time for KitKats.

That first month in country passed in a blur. We constructed living accommodation from the ground up, provided security for the detachment, in what was still a somewhat hostile environment, and helped wherever we could. The business of that first month, however, was short lived.

Having been on the receiving end of only the odd rocket and a mortar attack, I realised I would not see any real combat. Under-resourcing and managerial risk-aversion meant that me and the boys weren't even allowed out the front gates. So, what did we do? We did what all good airmen do, we sought adventure in mischief.

Recon Team in front of a Saddam portrait.

Around the two-month mark, the bosses decided to give us a Mule all-terrain vehicle or as it is known in the U.S, a 'Gator'. Unarmoured and looking like something straight off a John Deere showroom floor, the Mule drew derision from our US counterparts who were rocking armour, even inside the wire. Naturally, this vehicle had zero tactical application and was intended to be used by the security teams on their patrols, but we had other ideas.

With much planning and employing all we knew of military tactics, we instigated the first, and to my knowledge, the only Nitro Circus of Iraq.

We had a US mechanic trick up the Mule a touch and shed some of its weight with a gas-axe. In a secluded area away from the base and the prying eyes of the hierarchy, we built a racetrack incorporating berms, chicanes and even a rhythm section!

Time trials were on but to make things more interesting, we decided to have a buy-in. The original buy-in amount was a conservative $10US, but that quickly leapt to $100 as egos intervened in the winner-takes-all stakes.

The rules of the competition were simple. Multiple attempts were allowed up until the end of your deployment. You had to have one other person in the Mule with you. Times required verification from an independent member of another team. And drawing from the movie *Fight Club*, you do not talk about Mule racing!

Then, we discovered jumping. By jumping, I mean we would try to jump that Mule over anything, and guys even started taking shovels with them on patrols in order to build their own ramps!

While patrolling one shift, my section commander James and I discovered a perfect, natural jump over an aqueduct. We stopped the Mule, dismounted and scoped out Mother's Nature's answer to boredom that she had gifted us. After much discussion, involving complex trigonometry and speed-to-weight calculations, we nervously decided to give the jump a go.

Lap belts on, check. Helmets on and straps tight, check. Weapons secured and ready at hand (because after all, we were professionals), check. I told James he could drive, as he was the more aggressive of us and James had said confidently that he was willing to, 'drive it, like I stole it'. This was an attitude the Mule responded favourably to.

'Oh well, too late to pull out now,' I said, as the Mule left the ground at what felt like the speed of warp factor six. I don't recall much of the jump itself except for the weightlessness before gravity pulled us back to earth. What I do remember, though, is the interface between the sky and the ground.

*Snap* was the sound of my seatbelt breaking, hence, launching me skywards! Luckily, my second landing was better executed than the initial one and I managed to roll off the residual speed with only sustaining no more than some superficial scratches and bruises.

'Knighty, Knighty, you okay, man?' James yelled running over to me where I lay prostrate in the dirt. James thought he had killed me for sure.

James and I post mule jump.

I played dead for a moment but couldn't help pissing myself laughing. James joined in, relieved that he hadn't killed his mate but probably more relieved he didn't have to complete the required paperwork if I had been dead.

The Mule, however, hadn't shaped up as well as me. It never ran the same again and made a strange clunking noise whenever we pushed it beyond walking speed. It had though, given me some excitement on what was shaping up to be an underwhelming deployment.

After four months, our rotation was up and we were heading home. Apart from having been deployed with a great bunch of people and the hijinks typical of under-utilised troops in a war zone, I was starting to understand what little hope I had of seeing true combat operations if I remained as an airfield defence guard. However, a chance meeting with some private security contractors working in Iraq, along with a chat at their compound, would change the direction of things to come for me.

The Recon team end of trip picture.

# 4

# Schulzy

'Get in your bubble, Knighty,' my sniper supervisor calmly but firmly instructed me.

Bubble was a term used in our sniper section at 2AFDS. To be in one's bubble means to phase out all surrounding influences and noise and to concentrate solely on the task at hand.

I looked over at him. He had his usual cheeky grin which could only be described as amused. I knew there was something else about to be said, and so I waited.

'Don't fuck this up or you will be making the muffins.'

There it was, the comment I knew was coming. At the end of all our shoots, there was always a competition and, of course, in typical Aussie-male style, we made it interesting by having a bet. In our case, we had muffins as the wager. Loser of the competition would have to bake muffins for the whole recon/sniper section.

On this day, we were shooting on ranges of up to one thousand metres. I was the spotter and the sniper team were behind the rifle.

Normally, I would be on the rifle as I had the least experience. It was, however, decided that we, the newer guys, were going to get some time in spotting. As the spotter, I would be responsible for calling the range, making wind calculations and spotting swirl.

As the round leaves the barrel, it displaces the air in a vortex. When shooting across valleys or from elevated positions, spotting it is an important skill. Some days it can be easy and some days harder. Light conditions, temperature and humidity are all Mother Nature's way of affecting observation. In my case, I was inexperienced and frankly, I was just plain shit.

I'd missed seeing the swirl on the past two shots. We needed three out of the next five to hit the steel target sitting out at 800 metres or I was getting my Martha Stewart on. On a flat range, this generally shouldn't be too hard with a rifle that basically shoots itself. Today, however, we were on a field firing range and shooting from a position where our rounds travelled across two re-entrants before reaching the target. The wind was crossing in a different direction to its trajectory.

I made the correction from the last missed shot. In fact, I guessed, but I did not let anyone know that and the shot was fired.

'On!' was my call as I saw the round hit the steel target, waiting for the familiar *ting*.

'I jagged that,' I thought to self. The shot was a little high, so I advised a small correction.

'On!' I called for the next four shots.

'Ha, you got lucky,' the sniper supervisor chuckled.

'Nah, Sarge, never a problem, it was in the bag. I was just building suspense,' I answered. Truth be told, I did not see a lick of swirl. I did just get lucky, but no one ever knew that.

My sniper supervisor was a man named Wayne Schulz and I first met him in 2000. He came across as a stoic no-nonsense basic course instructor. His reputation preceded him as he was, at that time, the only qualified sniper within the ADG ranks. However, as time grew, I got to know him as someone who enjoyed a laugh and had a cheeky sense of humour. He became my mentor, confidant and most importantly of all, my trusted friend.

I have had a lot of trouble writing this chapter because Schulzy meant the world to me. I would not have got to where I did in the military without his influence and guidance.

I have spent countless hours trying to capture my raw emotions in words. Numerous phone calls have been made to the old recon/sniper boys and the infantry snipers who knew the man and held him in very high regard. I even had a former sniper reach out to me from the UK.

During these conversations, we discussed the importance of passing on stories and remembering the fallen. We discussed at length the good times, the bad times, the memories and the associated emotions. This verbalisation has been cathartic.

'What would Jesus do?'

Well, I don't usually ask myself that, but I do ask myself, 'What would Schulzy do?'

You know someone has really influenced you, when still after sixteen years since their passing, you find yourself asking what they would do if they were in your shoes? Wayne was my mentor, friend and surrogate father. For some reason, he didn't really like the name Wayne, and so he called himself John. Not that it mattered much because we usually just called him Sarge or Schulzy or Boss Hogg (amongst ourselves). I wish I knew who came up with the nickname Boss Hogg. We didn't call him Boss Hogg because he was a reflection of the namesake character from the TV series *Dukes of Hazzard*, oh no. He was quite the opposite, a type of authoritative figure and one to be unconditionally respected. Someone who was a true leader, a man who inspired and encouraged and maybe, because he might have carried just a tiny bit more weight than he needed to! I guess it was the backhanded compliment synonymous with good mateship, but there was never any doubt who was in charge, that's for sure! He was a strong and confident person and you couldn't help but listen.

I wasn't alone in having this sort of relationship with John, he had similar relationships with so many of his protégés/subordinates/peers/mates, whatever you want to call them. Which, on reflection, must have been all-consuming, especially, as he also had to balance his family life, just like the rest of us. Despite his hectic schedule, he always managed to give everyone the attention, encouragement or discipline they needed. With Schulzy, a spade was a spade, he didn't pull any punches and it was tough love or no love. He, however, had a way of speaking to you where it never felt like criticism and you always knew where you stood. It never stopped me and all his other protégés, trying to make him proud. Compliments didn't come all that often, but when they did you knew it counted.

At home, I remember him as an incredibly loving and doting father and there were no defences or walls up when he had his daughters around him. For a young man, this helped shaped me, learning that I didn't have to put walls up at home and I'm sure I'm a better father for it, given I didn't really have a benchmark until then.

I believe Schulzy was only the third qualified sniper ADG of the mustering, however, it had been many years between these qualifications and the mustering as a whole wasn't able to see past the qualification as a glory course/qual. This said, as the mustering moved away from hardened/dug-in defensive positions and inner perimeter patrols, the benefits snipers could bring were starting to be recognised. This recognition in the late 1990s is how I believe Schulzy found himself on the basic sniper course at 2RAR.

Airfields aren't small. A 2000-metre runway with associated airfield infrastructure and assets means an asset can be vulnerable over an expansive area. With all this space, airfields become highly susceptible to close target reconnaissance (CTR), observation and/or pathfinding if not properly defended. Schulzy was able to convince the chain of command that it simply made sense to qualify more snipers who in pairs could observe and cover the same area as a nine-man section (less the firepower, which was substituted for reach and early warning). Furthermore, a close target recon or observation was likely to be carried out by enemy snipers or trained recon elements and when dealing with these enemy elements, unless you get lucky, you need a sniper to catch a sniper. This wouldn't have been an easy sell, but he did it, and from the rank of corporal.

Schulzy was also a passionate ADG believer and for him, snipers gave the mustering credibility amongst the wider ADF, where the ADGs and RAAF, in general, were often used as a punching bag by the Army to make themselves feel better about their own shortcomings.

Ironically, this criticism never seemed to come from the infantry (it was usually non-combat corps that felt they needed to emasculate themselves). This was, in no small part, thanks to Schulzy who was well respected and admired within the closeknit community of army snipers. I can honestly never recall anyone talking about Schulzy in a negative fashion, such was his professionalism and personality. Not ever, although I'm sure he had the higher ups pulling their hair out occasionally, as his advocacy for his soldiers was second to none.

It was a three-year slog but in 2002, one sniper had been turned into nine. While ADG snipers do still exist, the traditional sniper cell seems to have faded. However, regardless of the new ADG structure, the RAAF should be thankful to Schulzy for making snipers a plausible, viable, and integral part of airfield defence.

In standing up for the section, he had his own unique way of doing things. Things that did not always make sense, however, Schulzy always had a solid explanation for.

He would advocate that the no.2 sniper should be the shooter, so that the more experienced no.1 could spot and better control the mission and its execution. I'm sure he'd have wanted the glory like the rest of us, but the mission came first.

He preferred a beret over a bush hat, and the uniform was always pressed and immaculate. Which in turn meant ours had to be too. He was the only bloke in the squadron to spit polish his boots, but he'd change them before going out bush.

> Below is a series of quotes from former recon/sniper boys: From about fourteen, I didn't have a father and without Schulzy I wouldn't be the secure, capable and confident person I am today. I owe him a debt I will never be able to repay and I'm sure I'm not the only one. The fact that a

man only eight years your senior can become a father figure speaks volumes about this incredible bloke. I still keep his number and email in my phone, I just can't bring myself to delete them. On one occasion, I wrote him an email that he'll never get.

\*\*\*

He called his rusted-out Gemini (that was Cynthia, Schulzys wife's first car, I believe) the 'Big Block'. I always found that a laugh. It was also hilarious watching this mammoth of a man squeeze himself into that thing.

\*\*\*

He fucking loved cake! Almost as much as he liked Jenna Jameson, which bordered on obsessive. I remember him loading me up with cash to buy him as many VHS movies of her as I could on a trip to the ACT one year.

\*\*\*

He was one of the most solid snipers I knew. He was intelligent and honest. I don't know why he never tried selection, but I suspect he didn't want to risk the failure, this is probably the only real chink he may have had in his armour; a fear of failure. I can understand that I guess when everyone expects you to be the best, that's a fair bit of pressure when Special Forces courses have such a high failure rate.

\*\*\*

I threw up all night (literally all night) on the day he died. From about five minutes after I got off the phone with Nathan, I couldn't control it, I was sick, so sick, to the point that I had nothing left to vomit, but the convulsions just kept coming for eight hours straight. I wrote him an open letter on a forum after he died, wish I still had it for you, there's probably some memory joggers in there too.

\*\*\*

His death may have saved my own. One week after he died, I got offered a job with ArmorGroup (maybe his) doing convoys in Iraq. He had helped me with my CV and organised the interview. Ironically, I didn't take it because he wasn't around to tell me 'Don't be stupid, the risk hasn't changed just because I got hit, you want this? Then just go and fucking do it!' I missed not having him around to help with that decision and many since. I also turned down a job with Dyncorp because of his death, but that job was guarding the new police academy in Kandahar, and that one probably would have gotten me killed!

\*\*\*

In 2003, the recon/sniper team won the military skills competition in Canungra. As a reward for dominating the rest of the sections, they were awarded with the first ADG rotation to Iraq. For some reason unbeknownst to all of us, Schulzy was overlooked for the sergeant's position. This gutted him. He had put so much work into the section and now his boys were deploying without him.

Utterly dejected and feeling betrayed, Schulzy decided to leave the airfield defence world. He had applied for the Queensland Police Force and was accepted. After finishing his cadet training, he was posted to a station in Cairns in far north Queensland.

Still wanting something more, he decided to apply for a contracting job in the ever-booming private world of contracting. Due to his work ethic and substantial resume, it was not hard for Schulzy to pick up work and commenced a contract with the now-debunked UK ArmorGroup.

Wayne was tragically killed in Iraq by a roadside bomb known as an IED. I had spoken to Schulzy not long before the mission and he expressed concern about how the company he was working for was putting them on the roads too early, before the US military had done their route clearances with explosive ordnance teams and vehicles.

He was running convoys at the time. I was lucky and only did the security detail work, but escorting 50 to 100 slow-moving trucks providing food and logistics to the US bases was dangerous work. The convoy teams were getting hit at an alarming rate.

I can't help but think where he might be now if he hadn't felt the need to leave. He definitely wasn't pushed out but by the time he left, I think he felt undervalued and, in my opinion, he was. Hopefully, now sixteen years on, his daughters can read this about her father.

Schulzy and I sharing a beer on a rest cycle whilst contracting.

# 5

# Up Close and Personal

Ripping the handbrake on and doing a 180 with the steering wheel, the car spun. I was not in a Matt Damon movie but on the illustrious Australian Military Police close personal protection (CPP) course. There is something cool about driving cars at Mach speed. We were driving them like we stole them.

The CPP course ran for six weeks out of Sydney's Holsworthy Barracks. The course taught a variety of skills from low-profile bodyguard work to high-risk protection, but my favourite part of the course was the driving component.

I stood there in my Gucci suit, laughing hard as I watched a guy sliding off the skid pan into the abyss. Don't worry, he was alright. In reality, we were taught safety first, oh, and how to look the part. I've always enjoyed the chance to wear nice clothes. This course saw us ditch our uniforms and instead, don our suits and dark glasses, cue the *Men in Black*. I was not wearing a Gucci suit. I wasn't even wearing one from Politix. My tight-arse was in a suit from Lowes. I still thought I was da bomb.

Unfortunately, the course content meant that I couldn't always get around Will Smith-style. I had the high-risk military side to learn as well.

Similar drills but with a lot higher profile standing. I was gunned up with helmet and body armour.

Reverse back to four weeks earlier and I was getting flogged on a preselection course. Funnily, I have worked out that everything in life is a selection process. Whether you join the military or have personal issues, you are continually growing through a selection process. There is no growth without suffering.

For me, at this time in my life, the suffering was physical and bloody physical. We ran the gas mask 2.4. In other words, we ran the stock-standard ADG fitness test but all in the service gas mask known as the S10 respirator. Ten minutes was the cut-off. Off course, only one or two of us made it and I definitely was not one of them. Failing did not matter on this occasion, this exercise was there just to test us, once again, replicating most things in life.

The final mission or test of objectives for the course involved three days of providing protection for an honorary colonel for the military police. There were overnight stays in various locations, planning routes and liaising with different companies and agencies about the requirements of our principal or the person we were providing protection for.

The principal would often go out to lunch or dinner, so it was the responsibility of the team to plan with restaurant managers about having a VIP inbound. The problem was, our client was not exactly important.

Using a lot of exaggeration and our military IDs, we had to tell some tall stories to these managers in order to obtain priority entry, seating, etc. This skill would be valuable later in life when I worked for a high-profile Hollywood couple.

One of the test objectives for the final exercise was for the bodyguard and security team to remain low profile and blend in with the crowd. In the fancy Sydney restaurants and bars, this was quite easy to do, as most people were wrapped up in their own world of high dining and talking about themselves.

Being part of the protective team, I sat down to eat my meal with NJ who was part of the protective team and the only woman on the course. The team leader planned for us to work together because nothing blends in more and does not raise suspicion than having a man and a woman eating a meal together.

We were situated closest to the principal and were primary to extracting the ageing client. The only problem was that the pretend principal was so chuffed at having a protective team, he would tell anyone who would listen. 'Fark me,' I thought, 'shut up!'

With the eagle-eyed instructors watching and assessing us from all angles, this was not good because we all wanted to pass the course.

After finishing his meal, it was off to the bar area where he was impressing his newly found female friend with stories of all his bodyguards.

The shit that was dribbling out of his mouth had me in stitches, but it seemed to be working on his female friend.

Several top-shelf scotches later, we were informed that we would suddenly be going to a chic Rose Bay bar in a Sydney ritzy area.

'Shit, a fastball!' I said to NJ (Fastball is an unplanned move).

We rushed like crazy and managed to get the advance team to approve the route and talk (or should I say, bullshit) to the management about the usual requests. No issues arose and our client and his new friend were ushered into a special entrance and given the preferential treatment. The female friend was certainly looking impressed by all this.

'Damn,' I thought, 'we are helping this guy to pick up.'

'Will I be dropping you back at home tonight or will you be catching a cab?' the primary bodyguard asked our principal's friend.

'She's coming home with me, matey,' was the reply by the principal.

The bodyguard put the call over the radio, giving us the heads up as well as our move time, in order to get the vehicles ready.

'Fuck me,' I said, shaking my head. I looked over to one of the other protective team and we just pissed ourselves laughing. 'Ah well, I'm sure the instructors will pull this up if needed,' I thought.

'Nope, go with the scenario unfolding,' was the call.

With this, we made the move back to our accommodation and handed two loved-up people to the astonished residential team.

'Enjoy, boys,' I said, as I did my handover to the residential team. My duty was done and I was off to get my beauty sleep. The unspoken number-one rule of being part of a CPP team is pretty much the same as the number-one rule of the Special Forces, look good.

The following morning, I rotated onto the advance team as I still needed to be assessed. It was the last morning of the course so we proceeded back to the military police barracks at Holsworthy.

True to form, it was on. I, like the other advance team members, were automatically taken out. My main test was for the protective team and bodyguard. After the shootout, I noticed the slightly hungover principal chatting to the members of the protective team. The principal looked as though he had not had much sleep. 'Old dog, sly fox,' I thought to myself, shaking my head.

This course went on to serve well, not only myself but many others. This qualification is held in high esteem for future employment as many of its students have moved on to conduct bodyguard work in Iraq and Afghanistan. Others went on to join the Australian Special Forces or became combat controllers like myself. NJ was contracted in Iraq as one of the few female bodyguards and is now a published author.

# 6

# A Very Pleasant Cruise

It was Boxing Day and I was on the cans with my ADGie mate Darren Hoare, when the call came in. 'There goes the cricket,' I said to Darren after receiving orders down the line. A magnitude nine earthquake had struck in the Indian Ocean, causing a 30-metre-high tsunami that had wreaked havoc on the shorelines of surrounding countries. To this day, it is still considered one of the deadliest natural disasters on record.

Banda Aceh, the capital of Aceh province in Sumatra, was closest to the epicentre and sustained the most damage with over 60,000 fatalities and many more people severely injured. As part of the Australian Government's contribution to humanitarian aid and disaster relief, a tri-service ADF detachment was promptly put forward and hence, I was about to be deployed to Banda Aceh.

This unexpected recall saw me quickly sober up, prepare my pack, radio and batteries for a C-130 Hercules flight to Darwin, the very next day. From Darwin, I then flew to Medan, the capital of North Sumatra. Twelve hours were spent in Medan before boarding another C-130 for the night move into Banda Aceh. During this time, we had been watching the local news and had seen the sheer devastation caused by both the earthquake and tsunami. We realised how underprepared we were for the task ahead.

The advanced force was already established when we arrived and they tasked us with providing aeromedical evacuation services at the airport since the group was mainly comprised of medical staff. The Army engineers that had also been on the flight were sent to the city to establish a fresh water supply for the locals.

Unarmed, me and eight other ADGies were tasked with the physical security of the airport. We also performed other ancillary tasks such as loading patients onto aircraft, unloading medical supplies and food, as well as assisting the doctors and nurses who worked tirelessly around the clock, treating patient after patient.

The engineers had established a clean water supply in town, so the boss decided to send a few ADGies to help. What I thought would be just handing out some water bottles, became one of the most humbling experiences of my life. I didn't just hand out water bottles, I assisted in the field hospital. The pall of death was barely masked by the sharp tang of disinfectant. The Acehnese patients, shockingly injured with amputations, burns and fractures, managed to maintain an uncommon humour and joy, even when presented with the loss of loved ones.

In the midst of such carnage, I witnessed one of the bravest acts I have ever seen.

Knowing that anaesthetic and pain medication were low, an Acehnese man volunteered to have his own irrevocably infected fingers amputated with no anaesthetic. Seeing an act like this made me question the medals that were often awarded after our deployments.

Troy and his section commander heading into the township of Aceh.

Standing next to a fishing trawler 6km inland from the ocean.

'Hi, apa kabar? (An informal Indonesian greeting for how are you)' I asked the friendly locals as they looked at Epps and I.

'*Baik baik saja,* (good, good)' they replied, smiling their large toothy smiles.

I was on a brief respite from the job, so Epps (another ADGie) and I had decided to hire some mopeds to investigate further inland. Riding south-west, away from the devasted city and into the breathtaking cloud-crested mountains of the Sumatran countryside, we unexpectedly met Ben.

Ben was a US F-18 Hornet pilot whose wings had been temporary clipped and so, like us, was out exploring the island. Ben had been tasked with coordinating the disaster relief effort of the USS *Abraham Lincoln,* however, as the massive aircraft carrier was anchored in

Indonesian waters, the Indonesian Government prohibited him from flying.

Ben must have taken a liking to Epps and I because not long after exchanging pleasantries and some deployment stories, us dirty and undoubtedly smelly Aussie ADGies got invited to spend the night on the mighty USS *Abraham Lincoln!*

Completely out of character, I actually asked for permission from the boss before accepting Ben's kind gesture. Ben allowed me to use his satellite phone and to my amazement and delight, the boss said 'yes.'

After spending weeks sleeping on the ground under flimsy mosquito nets, Epps and I were keen as, however, we still had to return the bikes.

'No problem,' Ben said casually, 'I will just send a chopper for you.'

Epps and I couldn't hightail back fast enough to return the bikes and right on cue, a US Seahawk helicopter materialised from the heavens and set itself on the airfield, just for us.

Epps and I strutted over, revelling in our moment of supreme importance, while a green hue of envy settled over the gobsmacked detachment.

It was a short flight to the carrier and there was a disconcertingly bounced landing, followed by an even more disconcerting reattempt. We disembarked the chopper and the memory of the landing was quickly forgotten. We had found ourselves in the land of milk and honey!

Milk and honey there was, but we smelled exactly like you would expect two men that hadn't showered in weeks to smell. But now, surrounded by inspection-level everything, there was an obvious and very stark contrast.

'How about we get you boys a shower?' Offered our new US mate, poorly concealing a smirk.

That long, hot, steamy drenching was better than sex. Yep, I said it and I don't take it back. Epps agrees with me on that one and no we didn't shower together, just in case that needed any clarification.

Now, smelling like milk and honey after our orgasmic ablutions, Ben presented Epps and I with flying suits to wear. The flying suits came complete with his squadron's designation and with patches with our names sewn on them! Epps and I looked at each other, both wondering how the hell he had managed to miraculously make this happen?

Up until that point during the deployment, I had only been eating ration packs, so you can imagine my delight when Epps and I were whisked off to the kitchen to have a meal specially cooked for us! Once again, the delight of sex is debatable against how good that meal tasted.

Swanning it up on the USS Abraham Lincoln.

Our boss had approved a no more than a 24-hour absence, but reverting to my more instinctive modus operandi vis-à-vis forgiveness and permission, the next two days saw us soaking up every minute while being treated like royalty on a cruise.

It was indeed a very pleasant cruise. I got to sit in the captain's chair, changing the words to the Kasey Chambers song 'I'll be the captain and you'll be no one', I sang to myself, thinking of the boys back on land.

Ben made sure we returned to the Banda Aceh detachment in style, just to help us rub it in that little bit more. We got to ride in the carrier onboard delivery (COD) aircraft, a transport supply plane launched using the very same catapult stream as the jets. This was a big deal.

The take-off was exhilarating and made even more pleasurable given the fact that only a handful of Australian pilots have experienced such a take-off. Now, after such a pleasurable experience, I fully understand the term pleasure cruise.

Security detachment for Banda Aceh.

# 7

# Contracted

'Fuck it,' I said to myself. 'I'm going to apply for a contracting job in Iraq and leave the military.'

It was late 2004 when I made this decision. The decision wasn't made in haste. Ever since first meeting private security contractors in 2003 on my initial deployment in Iraq, I had seriously considered leaving the Air Force and applying for a job. The fact that I had been provided with a tasty breakfast at their mess facility had pretty much sealed the deal, right there and then.

I knew I had a good chance of getting picked up by one of the private security companies, given my training and experience. I had previously attended the coveted military police close personal protection course and which the private security companies looked very favourably upon.

For a little over a week, we were given the pleasure of relearning how to drive and at times, drive extremely fast. This was all monitored and instructed by highly skilled individuals, some who were former race-car drivers. It took place in Canberra at a private company's establishment, complete with racetrack, skid pan and a variety of other obstacles, all coming together to make one very cool course.

Immediately after I had made the decision to give contracting a go, I managed to get some names and details of private security companies from my mate who was already working in the field. I dusted off the old resume and sent out some emails.

Just prior to Christmas, I received an email back from a British-owned company offering me a job. 'Well, this is easy!' I thought to myself. The kicker would be that I would be one of their new hires as they referred to us, and hence, I would not be hired until the new year. I was thrilled to have got offered a lucrative position straight up and the fact that I had to wait until the new year didn't worry me, as it meant I would be home for Christmas with my family.

Speaking of family, I may have made the decision to take on a whole new job in a Middle Eastern country, with the potential to get myself killed and no military payout if I did, all without consulting my wife. In all fairness, I had mentioned it the year before. That counts, right? Surprisingly, when I did finally tell her, she was cool with it. The money I would earn would allow her to be a stay-at-home Mum and relocate her home to North Queensland.

Christmas came and so did Boxing day and the new year, with the latter two spent in Aceh for the humanitarian mission Tsunami Assist.

Upon returning from the unexpected Aceh deployment, I immediately began my paperwork to discharge. In the Air Force, it's a three-month process. I figured the contractor hiring would be around that time, so best make haste.

'Shit,' I said as I ended the phone call from the security company that was to be my new employer. They had given me my departure date to leave Australia and it was within my discharge date, which meant I was still employed by the ADF. Lucky for me, I had annual leave up my sleeve and so I threw in my leave application, with the intention of never returning back from my holiday.

The new position required me to fly into Heathrow and stay a few days in London for the contract signing. I made the most of it and did a little touristy stuff. By day four, I was over sightseeing any more castles, chapels or churches. I just wanted to get to Iraq to commence my new employment.

After a few connecting flights, I landed in Kuwait. I was met by security staff there who whisked me away to an American base and onto a C-130 Hercules aircraft, headed for Baghdad International Airport.

'Man, its hot,' I thought to myself as I disembarked from the aircraft. I then laughed thinking, 'Of course it's hot, its Iraq.' I was suddenly taken aback at how much it had changed. It was a bustling metropolis of US and coalition camps. Iraqis had set-up businesses everywhere and it was a hive of activity.

We were met by the company's airport protective team. The airport team stayed at the airport and took care of the movement of clients and protective team members flying in or out of the country. I was to be working out of the Green Zone compound with most of the clients. The Green Zone was a safe zone in the dead centre of the city. Heavily fortified, it had been set-up by the Americans for their headquarters from where they would run the war, along with their diplomatic embassy and military units.

To get to the Green Zone from the airport, you had to travel down the dreaded Route Irish, which didn't, however, have the luck of the Irish. It was heavily laden with IEDs, vehicle-borne IEDs and had a plethora of locations to sight ambushes from. The road had taken many Iraqi and coalition lives, both military and contractor.

A member of the airport protective team handed me some body armour which looked remarkably similar to the eBay-purchased version that the reporter from the HBO mini-series *Generation Kill* wore.

'Any weapons?' I asked.

'You have me, laddy,' came the reply in a thick British accent as the contractor pissed himself laughing, before continuing, 'You'll get all the good shit issued at camp.'

***

'Yes, I am finally here!' I thought after my ID was checked at the military checkpoint. The drive down Route Irish had been, thankfully, rather uneventful and also done at a breakneck speed, weaving in and out of traffic.

That first day, I met my A-Team. The team leader was an exroyal marine, an ex-British paratrooper, a former Kiwi infantry soldier and yours truly. The dude with the thick accent hadn't been lying and I was issued the good shit. The A-Team immediately hit it off and we were keen as mustard to get the show on the road.

The A-Team set-out our own training schedule and as a bunch of international guys from all different military backgrounds, we worked well together and we were soon ready for our first mission. As the coalition had so wisely bombed Baghdad's electricity stations and water treatment plants, they now needed fixing. This meant they needed engineers, which meant it was now our job to protect the engineers.

First mission as a bodyguard.

I was elated to finally get outside the wire on that successful first mission. As a RAAF ADG, I did not get outside the wire. I completely missed World War Timor. Aceh was a humanitarian relief and in Iraq in 2003, we were not outside the wire, but there was this one time I was.

This one time at the airport, we were just supposed to help move some dignitaries and their equipment to one of the palaces that Saddam had built. They had their own protective team in one vehicle, one of our 4WDs and also our 110 Land Rover for the equipment and luggage.

I was driving the 110 Land Rover and I was in the company of a mate of mine MD, an air traffic controller. It was a move inside the airport and hence, did not require a security element.

As the convoy departed and passed the usual landmarks of blown-up Iraqi military stores, I noticed we did not make the usual turns.

'What the hell, MD? This is taking us to the main gate!' I questioned.

MD shrugged his shoulders, not knowing why we were headed in that direction.

Following the vehicle in front of us, we continued to the front gate checkpoint and proceeded through it, headed towards the palace that was not inside the airport, but inside the Green Zone. We drove down Route Irish, only the most dangerous road in the world. We were lucky though because IEDs had not really kicked off at that time. Only in Iraq!

\*\*\*

I hit an IED. Talk about taking one for the team, but the thing is, it was not even my team. I was helping another team. The bomb went off on the opposite side of the vehicle to me. *Kaboom!* But it wasn't really *Kaboom!* It was a small explosion and peppered the vehicle with shrapnel. Once again, luck was on my side as the device must not have been laid correctly nor did it explode correctly. I was still processing just what had happened, when I heard one of the more experienced guys on the team of contractors put out the call on the radio, 'IED, IED!'

The hit vehicle was an armoured LandCruiser. It was running, albeit slower, but it was still running. It had just survived the test! The bomb had blown out the tyres, but it was still driving on the run flats. Run flats are the hardened pieces of rubber on the inside of your tyres which allows you to drive on them flat. I commended the driver for staying on the road, I don't know if I would have done the same. The LandCruiser limped back into the Green Zone and got us back to our camp. We commenced our debriefing report process and I remember not feeling anything emotion-wise. It was as though the whole experience had been underwhelming.

\*\*\*

As life would have it, one of my last missions with the contracting company was into Sadr city. Sadr is Shia territory and heavily influenced by Muqtarda Al Sadr and his Mardi army. 'Great,' I thought, 'one of my last vehicle moves and it's into shit town.' My team leader had many years of experience in the country and had been to Sadr city, many a time.

'Lads,' the team leader piped up with his cockney accent, 'We run this a little differently. Once we hit the Sadr city district, we go into soft mode. No aggressive driving, keep looking out for threats, keep weapons out of sight and do not death stare anyone. Once we are at the power plant, long weapons stay in the car. The local cleric has guaranteed safe passage and reached out to us for help. These guys and girls, you just don't mess with. There will be egos and bravado with the young men there, but this is where we use our brains for this job. Load up the vehicle with extra water and a heap of food from our mess. We can hand that out as gifts.'

We nodded our heads, showing our understanding of the brief. The drive there was uneventful, but the atmosphere at the power plant was off the scale. You could taste the animosity and it didn't taste sweet, that is for sure.

The drivers stayed with the vehicles. This was for many reasons which I will now list. The primary reason was that we didn't want a bomb placed under them. Secondly, if we needed a quick getaway, the drivers would provide that. Third, the rifles were in the vehicles and the last and my personal favourite one, a vehicle is great as a battering ram, if needed.

As I escorted my engineer around the site, I attracted the attention of a young Iraqi male, no older than sixteen. He was armed with an AK-47 and scowled at me with a look of pure hatred. I will never forget that look, a child with so much built-up angst. The boy wasn't pointing the AK-47 directly at me, however, muzzle control didn't seem high on his list of priorities. Shitting myself, I thought, 'Oh well, here is my chance to use the soft approach, as my team leader so eloquently put it.

Reaching into my backpack, I grabbed a bottle of water and a Hershey chocolate bar. I gestured to him before throwing them over in his direction. They landed at his feet. The child soldier grabbed the Hershey bar and stuffed it in his pocket before throwing the bottle of water at me, just missing. 'Damn,' I thought, 'I have a livewire here.'

Moving away from the moody teenager, I walked up next to the client.

'How long do we have here?' I asked the engineer.

'About two hours,' he replied.

'Well, this is going to be an interesting two hours,' I thought, as we moved into the next plant room for the engineers to undertake engineering shit.

The job must have got boring for the young Iraqi security team AKA militia, and so he moved on and left me alone. I felt a big sigh of relief. The rest of the move through the power plant proved uneventful, and it ended with us thanking our Iraqi hosts and departing for our camp in the Green Zone.

The first contract had been enough for me to become a contracting slut. Before finishing that job, I was already pimping myself out to other companies for work. 'Score!' I thought to myself when I landed a contract with an American company, beginning January the following year. 'Christmas and New Year at home!'

***

'I could get use to this contracting,' I thought to myself, after landing stateside for the very first time in my life. I was at Fort Bliss in El Paso, Texas, to sign my new contract and to undertake some training. Fort Bliss is nestled right on the Rio Grande, a river separating the USA and Mexico. As someone who came from a sea-locked country, it fascinated me to look across the river and see a whole other country.

The town across the river from El Paso is Juarez. One of Mexico's sleaziest, murderous cartel-run cities, so naturally, I went there. As a new hire, I was only going to have a few days in the area, so I was going to make the most of it, while being stared at in Mexico like some sort of weirdo.

I was also able to experience the family restaurant chain, Hooters. Fun for the whole family, for sure. The fun of Hooters was then counterbalanced by having to endure the most painful transit travel experience ever, El Paso, Houston, Chicago, Heathrow, Dubai, Kuwait and finally, onto a US C-17 into Baghdad.

The new American company I now worked for ran the standard procedure that most companies did. They sent a team out to greet us and transport all of the new hires into the all-so-familiar Green Zone.

'That's cool, somewhere different,' I thought when in the initial briefing, I found out I was going to the Mosul team and would be leaving first thing in the morning. Travelling from Baghdad to Mosul could normally be achieved in five to six hours depending on military checkpoints, whether there had been any incidents or general traffic. However, my team would be travelling on Route Tampa, a notorious highway and we had to drop other members off at forward operation bases (FOBs) for their assignments to other teams. This meant our trip would take a lot longer than five or six hours.

Arriving in the early evening at my base, we unloaded the trucks, grabbed our weapons and met the rest of the team. It had been a big day and I was sleep deprived from the logistical nightmare that had been my flight itinerary, but I knew I had a job to get on with. My team's job was to transport and provide protection to the engineers and blow-up all Saddam's leftover ordnance. These storage facilities otherwise known as ammunition supply points (ASPs) had been bombed mostly by coalition aircraft. Some bombs missed their targets and some weren't completely destroyed. It was the engineer's job to destroy the leftovers. Local companies that had workers and plant equipment were employed to do all the heavy lifting, plus this lessened the chance of getting blown up, most of the time.

The ASP had been cleaned up within about six weeks due to the slick work of the engineers along with Iraqi help. News had come through that we were going to hang out in Baghdad, for a week or so, until our new base was built. 'Not a bad idea,' I thought when I was told that the security company and engineers had decided to build defendable living accommodation around the ASPs, to try to minimise time on the tumultuous roads.

The time had come for us to push south towards Tallil. We made it to Tallil airbase by lunch time. 'Beauty, just in time for a meal at the DFAC,' I thought, my stomach on my mind as per usual. DFAC is the dining facility, where they host every food known and for free! Also, the airbase was the home to the Ziggurat and being a history buff, this architecture fascinated me. Ziggurat was an ancient temple of sorts and built in 21BC. The original structure crumbled and fell apart, but it was rebuilt. Saddam had rebuilt the one I got to stand upon.

Staying only a few days, we pushed further south to our new home. My new home was basically an armed trailer park with re-enforced hardened structures to defend it from if needed. Everyone was allocated their accommodation and we got down to the important business such as discussions on where to put the gym, the making of a bar and building a recreation room.

Over the next few days, a few of the security team and I escorted our clients, the engineers, out to the ammunition supply point, so they could assess what needed to be done. I also met with our new interpreter Adnaan, who I would predominately work with. Even though I hadn't been with the company very long, I had been promoted to assistant team leader or 2IC as the term is used here in Australia.

As the newly appointed assistant team leader, I would be running the security operations at the ammunition supply points, leaving the team leader Chris to run the administrative and logistical side. He also dealt with employing local workers, plus communicating with company executives.

Work kicked off to a roaring start, then the roar changed to the type of noise you don't want to hear, rocket attacks. Adnaan explained to us that these random rocket attacks were the result of the company only hiring from one extended family and not another prominent family. It was their Iraqi way of telling us that we screwed up.

As Chris was away on leave, the responsibility now fell on me to try to get the arsenal sling stopped. I had Adnaan line-up a meeting with the disgruntled locals. We wanted the Sheik and his extended followers to come out to the site, but they would have no part of that and demanded we come to them. 'Ah well, so be it,' I thought.

'*Assalamu alaikum,*' (Peace be upon you) was said as we entered the meeting in the local town.

'*Alaikum salam,*' (and peace be upon you my friend) we responded politely.

Adnaan did all the introductions and small talk. Everyone was smiling and appeared happy, but I was still uneasy about it all. It was my first negotiation of such nature and I was trying not be nervous. I would later learn, through my training as a combat controller that fear is a normal emotion but panic is not. In the training continuum, you are taught techniques to control your fear. I wish I'd had it this day.

'No negotiations until we eat. The family has prepared a meal,' he informed me.

I nodded my head in understanding and thought, 'Okay, if I'm about to be on Al Jazeera in a jumpsuit getting paraded, then at least it will be on a full stomach.'

I definitely got a full stomach's worth, what a feast it was! The family had slaughtered a goat and prepared a massive tomato-based rice dish. Now, anyone who knows me knows I hate tomatoes but out of respect, I ate it all and it was one of the best meals I ever eaten, second only to that near orgasmic meal experience on the USS *Lincoln*. Given the chance, I will always eat goat. It tastes like lamb, only better.

Eating with the Sheik and immediate family trying to solve our incoming rocket problems.

In Iraq, with group meals like this, it is customary to eat with your hands. Well, your right hand. The hosts, however, held out spoons for us westerners, but we waved off the spoons and ate with our hands. I think our host got a kick out of this because we had shit all over us like toddlers with bowls of spaghetti.

With the feed finished, we set to negotiating. The sheik apologised about the rockets. He mentioned it wasn't ordered by him, but some younger Iraqis that were upset about not getting employed and he explained how unemployment was high and they had been hoping to get jobs.

Despite my initial nervousness, negotiations went well and we agreed upon the same deal with money and workers as the other family that worked for the company. With negotiations complete and a tummy full of goat and tomatoes, we said our goodbyes and headed back to camp.

The new group began working for us and everything was going well for about three days, then the families began to fight and threaten each other. I found it kind of comical, almost like a bad sitcom, but I knew if we wanted to get any real work done, we needed to come up with a solution. I sat down with the lead engineer and we figured out a plan. Together, we came up with the idea to split the families to either end of the supply points. This would require half the security to be with one family of employees and the other half of the security to be with the other family. In fact, the security was the easy part. I also had to stagger the start and finish times. Talk about logistics! I can now laugh at how combat operations can be a lot easier; you shoot or drop bombs on them and they shoot at you. Simple.

A week later, the team leader Chris was back from leave and it was my turn for some necessary R&R. The last month had worn me out mentally, but I had learnt some valuable lessons from it, such as how you can't place a western ideology on a different culture. I learnt that it is their right to live the way they want. If the families had their way, the day would start with a shootout, then some work and then finish the day with a punch-up. I'd had enough of domestic bickering, so I packed my bags and headed off on leave.

It was great to be home, spending time with my wife and my two daughters. I could tell they enjoyed having me home too. We spent the whole of my leave together and enjoyed a family holiday, laughing, playing and just being a normal family. I knew though, we were not a normal family. I wasn't a normal husband or a normal father. I didn't come home every night from working in the office or from the building site. I wasn't there to kiss my wife goodbye in the morning or my children goodnight in the evening. The normality of being an Aussie dad was in stark contrast to my role as a contractor in Iraq.

Returning from my leave, I arrived at Tallil airbase to be greeted by Chris and the other team members who I will affectionately refer to as the boys. The boys were like my family and, in all honestly, I had missed them while on R&R.

The drive back to the security point was a three-vehicle move. We had two teams at the camp for security, so this was a combined team convoy. As the team leader, I normally rode in the front vehicle, but because it was a combined team move, Chris and I rode in the rear vehicle. The other team's leader Jerry rode in the front vehicle.

'Dude, just let me ride in the front vehicle,' I complained to Chris. Chris then explained his reasons why I should ride in the rear vehicle. His reasoning was that whilst I was a team leader, quite often on convoys or other tasks, you can get relegated to other positions as the mission requires.

We departed Tallil for camp and an hour later, made our usual turn, off the hardball road onto the dirt track, which led us towards our accommodation. This dusty, bumpy track parallels a canal for six kilometres before making one last turn towards our camp. Due to the unforgiving terrain, there is only one way in and one way out.

*Boom!* Was the sound of the lead vehicle as it disappeared into a cloud of dust. We had set a pattern and the enemy knew it.

Immediately, standard operating procedures were actioned, with the middle vehicle pushing through to provide a support-by-fire team and the rear vehicle pushed up to assess the casualties and extract them.

'I want to get in there, let's go!' I yelled at Chris, my adrenaline pumping.

'No,' responded the skilled and experienced team leader. 'Let's just take a second to assess.'

His response was one of the best lessons I have ever learnt on military or military-esque operations. The man was gaining situational awareness and applying critical thinking.

After the assessment, Chris gave me the go-ahead and I drove next to the lead vehicle. I was nervous and asking myself many questions. 'Was there another IED? What state are the guys going to be in?' I pulled up next to the twisted molten mess that was once called an F250. It had stopped right on the edge of the canal. We trained to cross-load in between vehicles, thus providing protection and that is an excellent idea in theory, until the IED blast welds the doors shut. I could see the boys in the vehicle. Eric was in the back and he was moving slightly, however, Jerry and Rick in the front were motionless. 'Fuck,' I thought.

Without hesitation, I moved around to the open side, which paralleled the canal and I managed to pry open the front door. I triaged as best I could. I could see Eric was alive but barely conscious and had some wounds but no major bleeds. Jerry and Rick were unconscious, so I attended to them first. Rick had a pulse and didn't have any major bleeds. I leaned over to Jerry who had a sizeable hole in the side of him and I could not find a pulse. 'Fuck, Jerry is dead.'

Vehicle post complex ambush. The blast was that hot it welded the doors shut. This is the driver's side where Jerry was sitting.

Chris was on the satellite phone to the regional operations centre to organise a casualty evacuation and Shane the rear gunner, an ex-Marine scout sniper, had dismounted the vehicle and was providing cover.

I was talking to the conscious Eric constantly, while taking Rick's body armour off, to assess for wounds. Eric, to his credit, started to climb out the back window. He applied the rule that you are always in the fight until you're not. A true testament to his warrior spirit.

The actual side we hid to extract the clients due to the other side of the vehicle being welded shut. This exposed us to enemy fire. Eric's blood can be seen down the rear door where he climbed out.

I had removed Rick's armour and was assessing for wounds. He was still unconscious, but had a pulse which I could barely feel. This, I found out, later on in life, is not an uncommon presentation. I wanted to get Rick out of the vehicle and move him to a safer and less exposed location. The problem was that Rick was about 115 kilograms and I was standing on an embankment. 'Grab the stretcher and come give us a hand,' I yelled out to Shane.

No sooner had these words left my mouth, than insurgents from across the canal opened up on us with small-arms fire. Shane immediately returned fire. I spun around and returned fire. I didn't know where the enemy was, so I used Shane's fall of shot. The contact lasted for only ten seconds, but it felt like an eternity.

Once we had won the gunfight, I returned to treating the casualties. Eric had gotten himself completely out of the vehicle and was lying on the ground. 'Stuff it, I will get Eric to cover,' I thought, while Shane was busy getting the stretcher.

Approaching Eric, the extent of his facial wound became apparent. He was missing his nose, top lip and part of his tongue. Shane had set the stretcher up and I placed Eric onto it, providing cover between the vehicles.

Working in the South African anti mining vehicle in a high-risk area of Iraq

Chris informed us that team members and the medics were five minutes away and an Italian helicopter was inbound to transport the patients to the hospital at Tallil airbase.

Shane and I extracted Rick from the vehicle and placed him next to Eric. Rick was starting to come to. He had minor fragmentation wounds dotted along the side of his body, but I could see no further indications of wounds or internal bleeding.

I had upskilled in the US with a tactical medicine course and so I carried my own medical kit with fluids and drugs, but they were nowhere near medic standard. As we had our medical guys inbound, I thought I'd leave that to them, so I just monitored vitals. Both men were breathing and had blood pressure in the acceptable range for someone who has been blown up.

I moved back to Eric, trying to calmly talk to him. I had never seen a wound like his and I couldn't figure out how to treat it. I did my best and made sure the bleed didn't get worse and propped him on his side, ensuring he didn't choke on his own blood.

'Thank God for that,' I thought, when the medics and team members arrived and took over. The medics provided a higher treatment of care for the boys and the Italian casualty evacuation (casevac) helicopter came in and extracted them, except for Jerry.

The Italians, however, would not take Jerry as he was deceased.

'What the hell?' I questioned, 'What does that matter?'

Jerry was put into a body bag and we placed him into our coolroom for the night.

We drove in to Tallil at first light. After paying our final respects to Jerry, we handed him over to the US mortuary affairs team, who assured us he was in good hands and would be looked after.

A few months later, I ended my contract in Iraq. I was over it. 'You can keep this place,' I thought, but little did I know I'd be back.

# 8

# The Murder of Darren Hoare

Darren Hoare and I first met at our RAAF swearing-in ceremony in Townsville in 2000. Darren and I bonded from that moment, due to his overt larrikinism and our tendency to take the piss out of any situation.

Just sworn in, we were bussed to the airport, dressed in our most respectable trousers and long-sleeved button-up shirts. The accompanied ADF chaperone watched us both like a hawk, until we had safely boarded the flight to the Air Force's recruit training unit in Adelaide.

*Bing* was the sound of the service bell as Darren and I immediately buzzed the flight crew as soon as the seatbelt sign had been extinguished.

'Yes, can I help you?' asked the flight attendant.

'Sure can,' I answered. 'We'll have a XXXX Gold each, thanks.'

Darren looked at me and smiled, while the other recruits onboard stared at us in disgust. They all seemed to be cut from a significantly more puritanical cloth than Darren and I.

Not the XXXX Golds we were used to, but Darren and I drinking some borrowed CIA beers in Iraq 2003.

Hours and many celebratory beers later, we helped each other off the plane and into the fury of a small, round man that was to be one of our Air Force drill instructors. Not exactly sober, Darren said to me, 'He must have watched *Full Metal Jacket* one too many times.' I laughed and this secured our friendship, one that would last Darren's lifetime.

Throughout our careers in the RAAF, Darren and I followed in each other's footsteps. We roomed together during our recruit training and during our precious time off, we were often found at one of the shitty Adelaide pubs, drinking and having a punt on the horses. Following basic training, we were then posted to the same rifle flight with the Airfield Defence Squadron, being moved into reconnaissance and eventually, snipers.

Both Darren and I were deployed to Iraq and Banda Aceh together. We were known as the terrible twosome. The boys would say, 'Where one is, the other is not far behind and they will undoubtedly get into mischief, somewhere.'

Oh, how our wives would love us hanging out together. We would go to the shops to get milk and return hours later but with no milk and smelling like beer. I always thought it funny that the local Brothers Leagues Club never sold milk. That is something that Darren's wife still doesn't let me forget.

Ever the larrikin, the man always had a smart-arse comment and was not afraid to stir anyone up. I vividly remember him strapping on the boxing gloves for our infamous Jube boxing event. Now, Darren could not box for shit but was fighting another good mate who goes by the name Fatty. He was not known as Fatty because of his weight, but because of his red hair and a resemblance to Queensland rugby league great and media personality, Fatty Vautin.

The fight started and Fatty was not too bad of a puncher. He had been clocking Darren with a few good blows. Fatty then managed to bust Darren's nose and lip, and a bit of claret came forth.

This, however, did not deter Darren from stirring Fatty and giving him shit the whole fight, much to the amusement of the crowd. In the final seconds of the fight, Darren landed a punch on Fatty which sent Fatty's head back and produced blood.

There was no declared winner, but Darren still claimed the win, telling everyone, 'One punch is all it took.' I still smile when I think about how, for years later, Darren would sign off on an email with Darren 'one punch' Hoare.

\*\*\*

We had just returned from a night out at Penrith's notorious leagues club. We were based at Richmond airbase and my unit had been called up for a humanitarian mission in Africa.

Most of the days, while waiting to be deployed, had seen us do PT or shooting, as well as working on possible scenarios, because we were going to be deployed with an airlift transport squadron. Our job was to provide protection to the aircraft while they were on the ground plus also provide aircrew protection.

The job was dragging on and like most deployments, the longer you sit waiting around, the less likely the chances of it ever happening.

After a whole lot of 'hurry up and wait', most of us decided a night out to relax was required and to our delight, the boss agreed.

'You just have to attend PT in the morning,' the boss told us.

We all heard the boss's words, but the night may have gotten out of hand and we hit it pretty hard. After somehow getting home, I managed to set my alarm, sleep for a couple of hours and arise for a very dusty eight-kilometre run. That run was in fact, dustier than a rodeo. We were all a mess, well, nearly all.

As we were warming up, the boss noticed we were one man short.

'Where is he?' the boss asked, looking straight in my direction. Immediately, everyone looked at me. Thinking on my feet, I made up a story about Darren having a last-minute meeting with the aircrew.

'He will come back and brief you post PT, Boss,' I said confidently. As Darren was the section leader for that job, it came across as plausible and the boss bought it. That was, until Darren walks into view, still in his stepping-out gear. He had slept in and figuring he had missed us doing our PT, he had decided to venture out to get some greasy food from the on-base canteen.

Now, this would have been fine if we were not warming up about fifty metres away.

'Is that Darren and is he still in his clothes from last night?' the boss asked, raising an eyebrow.

Darren must have heard the boss because he immediately looked our way and recognised who we were. There was a stare-off for what seemed like an eternity and before the boss could get any other words out, he took off at the speed of light. It was one of the funniest things that I have ever seen and all the rest of the boys were in stitches.

'Go get him, Knighty,' came the stern order as we all pissed ourselves with laughter.

I managed to pull myself together as I jogged over to a bush to find a very hungover Darren leopard crawling in jeans, a button-up shirt and very nice leather shoes.

I smiled to myself, left Darren in the bushes and ran back to the group. 'I can't find him, Sir,' I said trying not to break into laughter.

'I'll catch up with him later,' the boss responded.

The rest of the run was brutal but made a lot easier by the fact that Darren had provided us with amusement that would last us a lifetime.

I do not know what it was with the mateship that Darren and I had with each other. I do, however, know it was very special and one for which I am forever grateful, despite it being cut so short.

'No way! Who knows, what you lads will get up to,' was the usual reply whenever we asked to work together. This, however, never stopped Darren training me. After I failed my first sniper course, he spent time teaching me the ways he used to shoot, move and stalk a target. He spent hours teaching me how to observe unnatural objects in the field. He was always keen to help a mate and pass on his knowledge.

\*\*\*

In 2005, during my contracting time in Iraq, I impressed Darren with my tales of the rockstar lifestyle and the money I was earning. So impressed was he, that he quickly followed.

Darren, always the skilled operator and a highly regarded leader, was quickly promoted to a site security manager's job in southern Iraq with ArmorGroup UK. He and his family breathed a sigh of relief as it took Darren off Iraq's still-deadly streets and beyond the crosshairs of Muqtarda Al Sadr's Mardi army. Chatting with those that were there at the time, all agreed Darren was excelling as a manager.

On 9 August 2009, Danny Fitzsimons, a loose cannon with a criminal record for weapons charges, with known psychological issues and no possible justification for being anywhere near a security contract, had somehow managed to weasel his way onto ArmorGroup's books.

Fitzsimons was drinking loudly in the company of another contractor Paul, in the security company's compound in Basrah. Darren was concerned for the company's reputation, given that the client's accommodation was within earshot, and he entered the room to quiet the lads down. A heated argument ensued, followed by a fistfight that ended in multiple gunshots being fired.

The gunman Fitzsimons fled the room, pursued by other contractors. In an attempt to escape, he shot an Iraqi guard in the leg before being overtaken by contractors and guards and then being subdued by the Iraq police who arrested him. Back in the compound's room, Darren and Paul both lay dead from execution-style gunshot wounds to their heads.

During his trial, Fitzsimons attempted to plead insanity and speciously claimed self-defence, both arguments being summarily rejected by the court. He was convicted of murder and sentenced to 20 years in an Iraqi jail. Eleven years into that sentence, he was extradited to the UK where he remains in prison.

Writing is cathartic and I had hoped that writing about the murder of my best mate would be some sort of therapy for me. I feel guilty because I was the one who introduced him to the world of contracting. I can't honestly say that writing this has freed me from that world of guilt, but with as much rationality as I can muster around this topic and by way of honouring his memory, I strive daily to remember that Darren lived his life on his own terms and followed me to Iraq with his eyes well open.

**For Darren,**

*Darren, mate, I haven't completely processed your loss and I probably never will. Certain smells, the passing of anniversaries and the smallest of events that recall our shenanigans together, still render me an emotional mess. Even though I'm not a superstitious man, I'm certain you've been watching over me in death as you did in life. Through the numerous scrapes that have ensued in mine, I know you've guided the hand of fate. I write this book as much for you, as for myself.*

Darren on patrol in BIAP 2003.

Darren and I on drinks break during our boxing day front yard test.

# 9

# Pirates and Kiwis and Seals, Oh my!

'Matty, I don't know boats and my only knowledge of piracy comes from the movie *Pirates of the Caribbean*.'

My mate Matty laughed down the phone line, 'You will be right, mate,' he assured me. 'There is a solid crew on board here including former Kiwi SAS and some royal marines. They will show you the ropes. Also, I have vouched for you.'

After eighteen months contracting in Iraq, I'd had enough. I had farmed my resume out to other companies, pimping for jobs in Afghanistan, Europe, South-East Asia and also out to the United Nations. I was short-listed for a gig in Afghanistan on the poppy-eradication program and I was also offered a job in France. The Afghan job was shit and the French job came with too many complications.

Then Matty, who I had worked with in Iraq, reached out to me. He offered a job doing anti-piracy work in South-East Asia. I had no experience with boats or this line of work, but like many things in life, it's not what you know, it's who you know.

'It's good cash, Knighty, 'Matty said to me. 'We are working out of Singapore and all we have to do is babysit this cargo up the Straits of Malacca.'

'Where the heck are the Malacca Straits?' I asked myself, not wanting to sound like a geographical dumb-arse in front of my friend.

After the phone call, I sipped on my after-dinner Negroni and conducted some research. I found out the Straits of Malacca are a major shipping channel between Malaysia and Indonesia. It is one of busiest shipping lanes and from an economic and strategic perspective, one of the most important.

The Straits of Malacca was also known for its piracy. In 2004, it accounted for 50 per cent of the world's piracy. By the time I worked there in late 2006, it had dropped to about fifty acts of piracy for the whole year.

Still sipping on my Negroni, I thought, 'Oh well, let's give this a crack, off for another adventure.'

A few days later, I was sent my contract by the company's management. It was a one-off gig and would last for only four to eight weeks in duration. A company was setting-up an exploration mining rig in the ocean. Well, that is what I was told.

As I was perusing through my contract, it had the usual paragraphs about pay, meal allowances and accommodation, but something was missing, nothing about flights to Singapore.

I wrote an email to human resources asking about flights and dates for commencement of work.

'Oh, you book and pay for your own flights. Just get here as soon as you can,' was the email response from HR. I drafted another email in response, 'Like hell I do, I do not pay to come to work!'

My assertiveness prompted a little action because I had the operations manager ring me.

'Kia Ora, bro,' he greeted me. 'That is just the standard contract. I will have the new contract written up and sent to you paying for your flights. You just book them and we will pay. Look forward to meeting you.'

There were no ill feelings on my side, I understood that companies will always look to make a buck or cut corners when needed, however, just because I had zero experience in the maritime world did not mean I was paying for a return ticket to Singapore around Christmas time.

***

'What the fuck do you want?' questioned one of the largest Kiwi men I had ever laid eyes upon. I had buzzed the door of the Changi hotel where the team was staying, excited to meet my new workmates.

'I'm, um, um...' I stammered, shitting myself.

The Kiwi giant laughed and cut me off, 'Just fucking with ya, cuz! You must be Troy. Come on in,' he smiled, with a huge beaming smile.

I smiled back, feeling a weight lift from my shoulders and I followed him into the room.

'I am George,' the giant told me. 'You come highly recommended from Matty. You better not stuff up, ay!'

I looked at George and he started to piss himself laughing again before giving me a slap on the back which, in all honesty, almost sent me flying, even though it was meant to be friendly.

George introduced me to the crew. There was a lot of chat and good banter going on. I was told I would be rooming with Steve. Steve was an ex-royal marine and the most experienced in these over-the-water operations. He was also the team leader. Steve had worked on what the Brits call The Circut, household bodyguard work for rich families throughout Europe. He had also contracted in Iraq, Afghanistan and done an anti-piracy operation around the horn of Africa. 'Another good crew to work with,' I thought to myself.

My mate Matty was out on a ship with his own team, escorting the first shipment of cargo up the straits. While I was still on land, Matty would email back nightly situation reports. I remember him writing about how rough the seas were and the fog that set in, reducing visibility and hence, making it dangerous for shipping. I had no idea about these things and I would turn to Steve and ask a million questions.

I spent the five days prior to boarding the ship, performing rehearsals, buying stores, meeting the captains of the ships and naturally, gorging myself senseless with delicious Singaporean cuisine.

It was now my time to start the cruise and I was partnered with Steve the team leader. We were on the chase boat or intercept craft, which was a fast vessel in the flotilla and it was at this time, I met Jotpoh. Jotpoh was a Thai Navy SEAL. He was a really solid hand, who, besides being former Thai Special Forces, could also translate.

Because of licensing regulations and being foreigners, we did not have weapons. To counter this, the company hired a Malaysian security company to provide us with armed guards. 'This is going to be interesting,' I thought, chuckling to myself.

We disembarked and steamed north, towards our first port of call. I have no idea what it was called, but we arrived at O'dark 100. Upon docking, Jotpoh jumped off the ship and went to round-up our guests. This was not his first rodeo. He had worked for the company before and knew the drill.

Rumour had it that this was a new Malaysian security company. They had undercut the previous company, dollar-wise. I could hear Jotpoh yelling and he later told me he was telling them to hurry up. 'I like this guy already,' I thought.

The lead guys were carrying the weapons and ammunition. Steve and I were directing them where to store the weapons and ammunition, when we heard a splash, followed by another larger splash. We then heard what can only be described as squealing and screaming.

'What was that?' I asked Steve.

He didn't answer but instead, jumped onto the jetty and headed towards the noise. I followed him fast.

Arriving at the scene, we saw a Malay security guard in the water and Jotpoh saving him. The Malay security guard had fallen into the water and Jotpoh had jumped in to save the squealing, splashing man who couldn't swim. Steve looked at me and with his British accent said 'Fooking hell, mate, what have we got ourselves into here?'

At that point in time, the old saying came to mind, 'If you pay peanuts.'

Once everyone had boarded without ending up in the water, we set sail for the straits to rendezvous with the cargo ships. Along the way, Steve showed me the ropes about what the radars did and how they worked. He questioned me on our standard operating procedures and educated me about the law at sea. I felt like I was back at school, but this was a school I liked and so I soaked it all in.

Steve and I would split the watch, sitting on the bridge with the ship's captain. I used to practise my Bahasa Indonesian with the crew. The ship was an Indonesian-owned craft and crewed mostly with Indonesians.

Besides intercepting a couple of harmless *sanpans*, it was an uneventful trip. A *sanpan* is like a skiff. These crafts, however, had high-powered motors and are the craft of choice for pirates in the area.

The guys we intercepted on these *sanpans* were just hawkers from some local villages on the mainland. Most of the villages are poor and hawking is a way to earn extra money and put food on the table for their families, so I can not begrudge them for that. The *sanpans* hang out in the channel with cheap smokes, pirated DVDs and other junk. One guy was trying to sell 'original' Rolex watches and suits. 'Yeah, right buddy,' I thought, laughing to myself.

Dropping our cargo ships off at their destination in the Andaman Sea, we headed for home.

'Let's crack these shottys out and shoot some off this rubbish in the ocean,' suggested Steve. We were halfway home and looking to get in some range time. The unfortunate thing about the straits is that it is littered with rubbish.

Teaching our Malaysian security guards how to shoot.

I nodded my head, happy at his suggestion, however, I didn't have any hearing protection so I stuffed my ears with toilet paper to try to block out some of the noise. I remember thinking how I wasn't going to lose my hearing out on the ocean. Little did I know that four years later I would lose significant hearing in my left ear from gunfights in Afghanistan.

Conducting shotgun training. Note the toilet paper as hearing protection.

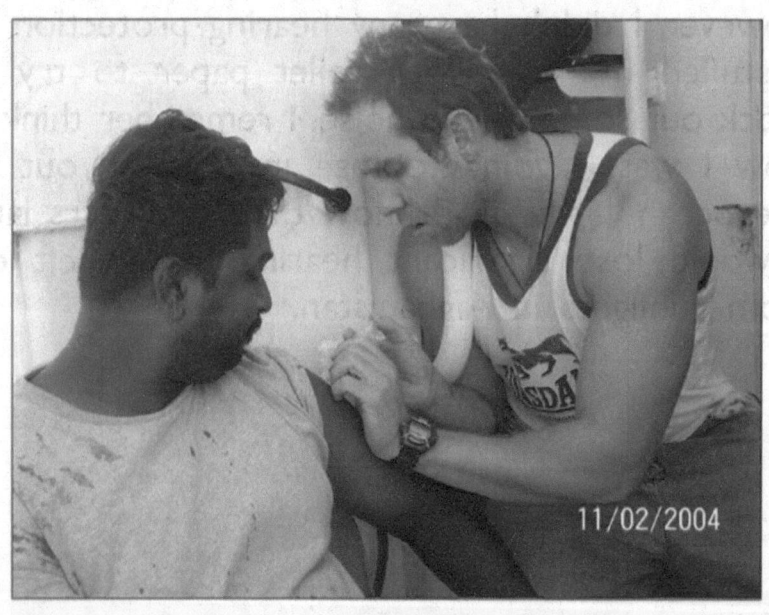
As team medic I had to quite often administer anti-nausea drugs.

As we neared the southern end of the straits, the ship came to a grinding halt. The tired crew started yelling in Indonesian and tempers were flaring. I gave a puzzled stare in Jotpoh's direction, and he explained that something was caught in the props.

The first mate had been at the helm and was now receiving a bollocking from the captain. The ever-calm Jotpoh walked over to the captain and gave him what I assessed to be a, 'Shut the hell up.'

*Splash* was the sound of Jotpoh diving into the water, again. He had stripped down to his shorts, grabbed a mask and knife out of his bag and dove into the water to take matters into his own hands.

'Shit, Steve, he has been down there a long time,' I said, worried about my Thai friend.

'He knows what he is doing,' Steve assured me.

After what seemed like a very long time, Jotpoh surfaced, holding a large chunk of fishing net. We helped him back onboard where he proceeded to chastise the captain and wave his hands around a lot. As he walked past me, I asked Jotpoh 'What was that about?'

'Fucking idiots,' he said in his heavily accented English, smiling. Steve and I couldn't help but laugh.

# 10

# Nasi Goreng

Happy to be home from my time on the high seas, I sent my resume off to a number of international companies, because I was now unemployed. While waiting for another dream job to just fall into my lap, I took on a local, normal civilian job my father-in-law had hooked me up with. For the first time in my life I thought, 'Wow, I have to work for a living.'

Luckily for me, working for a living didn't last that long, because an appealing job offer came through from an Australian-based company. The offer was for a security manager's job working for a smelting company in Indonesia. I won't lie, I was pretty euphoric at this, as I was getting bored with being home. I loved spending time with the kids, but I was getting antsy for adventure and my wife could see it.

'Troy, you need to head back overseas,' she told me. 'I'm getting sick of your grumpy arse.'

She was right, the routine of everyday home life made me a grumpy arse. I loved spending time with my children, but adventure was like a drug for me, it was addictive.

I had a phone interview with one of the company's directors and a day later, I had the job. Not long after that I was on a plane to

Jakarta. I was semi-familiar with Jakarta, having passed through there on the way home from Banda Aceh. I could speak a little Bahasa Indonesian to impress the locals, but I was still the *bule,* the term they use for outsiders or white people.

I arrived at the hotel and what a hotel it was! 'Five stars, yeah, baby,' I thought to myself. For someone, who apparently loved sleeping under the stars, I didn't mind sleeping under only five. I had a deluxe room and everything I ordered or drank went to the room and was billed back to the mining company. Working for a multibillion-dollar mining company, this was chump change.

Several kilograms later, it was time to work. In usual fashion, I had drunk the hotel almost out of beer and ate them out of *nasi goreng istimewa.* First stop was some mine in the northern Island of Sumatra. The place was massive. Part of my job was to oversee the training plan of the local *satpam* or security. Upon arrival, I had not entered a shitstorm, quite the contrary. The contract had been going on for some time and my predecessors had done an excellent job.

I took over the job from a highly intelligent former paratrooper. He was a 3RAR veteran and gave me a solid rundown of the land. I was most appreciative of the comprehensive handover and for not being just tossed into an unfamiliar operating environment.

The job was certainly not the high-speed life I was used to, but I certainly still enjoyed it. It gave me a new opportunity, an opportunity to use my brain rather than just my grunt. I had to analyse theft reduction, create plans to keep illegal smelters from emerging on the mining corporation's land and most of all, keep the directors happy. I learnt things like SWOT analysis for the mines, strengths, weakness, opportunity and threats. It was a time of true evolution and growth for me, however, I still missed the action.

They say money makes the world go around and this is certainly the case in Indonesia. Gratis payments, they call them. Westerners might call them something else, but hey, who am I to judge? My time in the Middle East had taught me that. Gratis payments were necessary and expected, so every so often, I was given a suitcase full of money and off to the local police chief or an Indonesian general I would go. I would hand over this suitcase stuffed with money and, in exchange, they would help us out with any criminal activity on mining company land. Business done Indonesian-style.

I was dropping off a gratis payment to the local commander, when he suggested I come out to their range for a shoot. They had recently built their own range and he was quite proud of it and wanted to show it off. 'Why not?' I thought to myself. 'Some trigger time is always soothing for the soul.'

A quick photo with the local TNI commander I had to visit for his monthly gratis payments.

'OK,' I said, accepting his offer.

'*Hebat!*' he exclaimed, happy to get the chance to show off his new pride and joy. The commander went on to tell me that me and my counterpart would ride with him.

'What?' I asked my Indonesian counterpart, who was laughing hard as we climbed into the vehicle.

'You will see,' he answered, smirking.

Many hours of travel later, we were in the middle of the jungle rolling up to the range. The Army had bulldozed around 100 metres by 50 metres of land. Targets were up and the Indonesians were blasting away. I looked at my counterpart and he was still grinning and I had no idea why. Was it a personal joke I just didn't get?

'Funny range, hey?' he finally said to me, laughing.

I didn't think it was funny, it was a range and I was happy to finally get in some range time after a dry spell away from hot brass. I told him my thoughts, 'It works mate, that's all that matters.'

Conducting shooting with the local TNI.

I had a great time and it made me realise how much I was missing so many things about military life. It hadn't been long before that I had started to hear rumours that the Australian Air Force were going to put forward a special tactics project. I had scoffed at the idea and returned to my life of luxury, eating awesome food and drinking beer.

The special tactics idea gained traction and before long, I was hearing about the first guys beginning their training. This spiked my interest and I was secretly jealous. I wanted to do that. I wanted in. I wanted to be special. My mother had always told me I was special, but that didn't count. I did, however, have a contract to fulfill and I was going to honour that. 'Once the contract is over, you can reassess your options,' I said to myself.

What's funny or ironic or maybe, just the way the universe works, is that during my time in Indonesia, some of the boys, I would end up deploying to Afghanistan with, in the not-too-distant future, were working only a few hours away from me in East Timor. They were there trying to capture the rebel leader Alfredo Reinado.

Below is an extract from a good friend of mine Murray from 2nd Commando Regiment who recounts his experience in East Timor. Murray went on to guide and mentor me throughout our Afghan operations.

> Operating in a jungle environment and understanding just how it can literally come up and bite you if you're not careful, careful planning, combined with body and equipment preparation, will ensure you give yourself the best conditions to be able to successfully soldier in this harsh

environment. This set us up for planning and execution for Afghan down the track.

I deployed to East Timor in November 2006 for a six-month tour. I was set and understood what to expect, from the environment, anyway. What I did not expect was how unpredictable the government conditions were and what our mission would really be. East Timor or Timor-Leste was again reignited into chaos during 2006 when Alfredo Reinado escaped from prison and then proceeded to drive continuously around East Timor with his rebels and taunt the government.

My unit 4RAR Commando back then (Renamed 2nd Commando Regiment in 2009) sent over a platoon-sized group to track and report on his position. My platoon replaced that element in November at the Dili airport and then we began driving around the entirety of East Timor and reporting on Alfredo. The government could not seem to decide on exactly what they wanted from us. We were told to report, do not arrest, communicate, seek his intentions and then release him. Do not block him and put him into a position where he would respond with violence.

The whole situation was crazy, there were days when my platoon would catch up with him and his 10 to 15 rebels, share coffee and chat about the weather. Other days we were ordered to 'shape' his movements and potentially coordinate and arrest.

However, little did we know, he was reporting to the government behind our backs and smoothing things over from time to time. The whole dynamic was very frustrating and yet slightly amusing. I mean, hey, we were on operations, getting decent pay, working out and assessing the news posted to the platoon in a benign environment; it definitely could have been worse.

Alfredo seemed to be visiting the town of Same quite a bit. Every few weeks, he would stay with his men on the hill overlooking the town . That is where we met for coffee most times and to be honest, I didn't mind him. He was friendly, polite, passionate about his country and its future and didn't seem too concerned with us.

One morning, he took his convoy and headed south to Suai. Soon after, I was ordered to take my team up to the compound on the hill and get some information about it and take photos of the area.

The search and reporting continued until 25 February 2007 when the rebels and Alfredo raided a police station. They stole radios, assault rifles and pistols. This was the final straw, the government had enough and he was considered a higher and more realistic threat to the stability of the government and the country.

Another platoon and some special air service regiment patrols were flown in at short notice and we began planning for an assault on whatever location he picked next. He settled back on the Same compound and we immediately cornered off the hill with armoured personnel carriers and infantry.

All the team commanders, platoon commander and platoon sergeant started our planning cycles and rehearsing who was doing what and which support elements we had. Sergeant MH and his platoon had just returned from rotation three in Afghanistan. Sergeant MH is a particularly good friend of mine and we grabbed some coffee, sat down and discussed assault options for this compound, finally deciding on his platoon fast-roping onto the target, simultaneously, as my platoon conducted a ground cordon and assault after walking onto the target from about five kilometres away.

While the 2nd Commando platoons and SASR element were discussing options, I flew in a Huey with a Timor Government official and a senior SASR-warrant officer up to Same, for one last negotiation with Alfredo. We landed, turned off the helicopter and walked to the compound, however, I remained outside of the room where the meeting took place. On the flight back to Dili, I asked SASR Warrant Officer F how it went and what was the outcome? 'Not good' was the reply and from that point, I knew the job was on.

The walk up the mountain to our assault positions started at about 2000 hours, and we arrived at about 0100 hours with that walk to target being one of the most arduous I had ever done. I was absolutely spent as I moved into my final assault location.

We could see and hear the Orion surveillance aircraft circling overhead with one of our assaulters inside (providing information about the ground assault force to the pilots and surveillance operators). H hour was set for about 0130 hours.

Totally exhausted, we moved to the edge of the wooded area and observed three rebels patrolling the road. They were about 20 metres away and to be honest, I was totally surprised they couldn't hear the last remaining assaulters climbing up the cliff and getting into position. It was just then we heard Sergeant M's Black Hawks flying in on final and then start roping, the code word to start the assault was given and we all moved off to our assault and block positions.

Teams were making explosive entries, while others were still roping down from the Black Hawks and my team was patrolling across to the other side of the compounds to our entry point. Explosives, flash bangs and helicopters were drowning out the radio chatter and it was hard to hear who was doing what. We knew there was about eight rebels on target but didn't know any locations and as we were reaching our team's entry point, a rebel ran out about 15 metres in front of us and shot several pistol rounds at us and before we could return fire he took off around the corner, unslung his rifle and gave a burst at the Black Hawk that contained some snipers. One was hit with bullet fragments as it just missed his head and exploded on the bulkhead so the door gunner let rip with the Mag 58 (7.62 mm heavy machine gun) and killed the rebel. There was firing coming from both north and south and a few grenades exploded also, and the assault was over relatively quickly. Within 30 minutes or so, we had accounted for five dead enemy and nil friendly KIA or WIA, so an awesome result, however, once we consolidated and team commanders came together, we learned that none of the dead was Alfredo and he had slipped the cordon with another two rebels.

We didn't have the assets or manpower to track him that night and we would have to wait. Having a UAV (drone) and a JTAC to coordinate the Black Hawks and the Orion would have been exactly what we needed as thermal and infrared cameras mounted on a UAV that is coordinated through a ground call sign is invaluable and this was a lesson for our upcoming Afghanistan tour.

It was now about 0300 hours and we had accounted for all teams and equipment. We now began searching and accounting for the five dead rebels and their fighting equipment, laptops, vehicles and personal gear. By 0400 hours, all searching was complete and we actually got to sit down and rest. The two days of planning and rehearsing the mission, combined with the five kilometres uphill to the target, mixed with the adrenaline rush of the assault, caused me to sit down and instantly start falling asleep. I had to continuously shake myself and stand up for that last hour, otherwise, I'd have totally fallen asleep on target. This was one of the first times and there would be many more. I understood there becomes a point after days of limited sleep, long and arduous insertions followed by the excitement of combat that the body can really fatigue and you can become un-operational. Adrenaline and motivation are not a wonder drug that gives you endless power; your body and mind at some stage will shut down.

So, there we go, two men kicking around within miles from each other in the jungles of South-East Asia who, years later, would be side by side fighting in Afghanistan. Speaking of the universe and bigger picture shit, I did not have to wait for my yearlong contract to finish. The smelting corporation had a hostile takeover and the new company did not like us *bule*.

'A bit racist,' I thought laughing to myself when I was told my contract was ending. Truth is, they were probably right. God knows what my room charges were like at the end of my stay? 'Well, there you have it,' I said to myself, 'let's give this special tactics project a shot.'

# 11

# Selected

In 2008, after three years on the contractor gravy train, I jumped off. I landed back on base, returning to full-time service with the Royal Australian Air Force.

To be honest, upon my return, I was technically still in the Air Force Reserve, until I had proved I had what it took to pass the elite Commando selection course and reinforcement cycle (REO) for the RAAF's new combat controller air specialist courses. I thought I knew what I was in for, but little did I know that I was about to discover what mud really tasted like.

Still looking for adventure, I thought this new role would feed that insatiable appetite of mine. I was also very much aware that I wasn't getting any younger, so after hearing rumours the year before, that something called the special tactics project had been proposed at the RAAF Base at Williamtown near Newcastle, I decided this could be my one-way ticket to Adventureland.

Reaching out to a good mate and mentor of mine, I mooted the idea of returning to the fold. He and the CO pulled some strings for me, while I blew the dust off my old uniform and got the iron hot, ready for a big demotion.

The idea behind the project was to create a squadron of special operations airmen to emulate the US Air Force's Combat Controllers (CCTs). We were to be air integration specialists, sufficiently skilled as to enable our deployment with Commando (Special Forces) elements on operations.

This project, like every new project, had teething problems and there was a distinct lack of numbing gel to be found. A disheartening budget cut had been caused by a change in government. Despite being under-resourced and beset by naysayers, the project had the faith of the true believers, the grit of those long accustomed to kicking against the pricks and so we cobbled together a program and cracked on with the mission.

Later that year, the project graduated its first combat controller (CCT), known as HR, who was immediately deployed to Afghanistan with the 2nd Commando Regiment. Still in training for this gruelling selection course, HR was a source of inspiration for me, his example making me dig deeper and train even harder. According to our commando brethren, HR was 'killing it', and so our hearts were full of pride!

Naturally, only three weeks out from the start of the selection course, I contracted a virus. It felt like I had been hit by a bus! And it was not only that infamous man-flu strain, I will tell you now, it wasn't! I don't remember the exact diagnosis from the medical officer, but it most certainly wasn't man flu. I was administered fluids and medication and, in the interests of other selection candidates, I was put in an isolation ward.

'No way!' I politely replied to the hierarchy, who were seriously suggesting I reconsider my plans to go on the selection course. It was now only three days until the start of course and two weeks since I had contracted the dreaded lurgy. I had lost six kilograms and a lot of my strength with it. I was doing what I could to gain weight and some strength, eating everything in sight and focusing on rest and recovery. 'Strap in, Troy,' I thought to myself the day before selection, 'this is going to be one hell of a ride.'

Day one of selection saw me cause the entire course to have to do a whole heap of push-ups. You see, the course began with a kit inspection, to see if one can follow orders and I cannot.

'You fucking soft RAAFie, why don't you just quit already?' screamed an instructor at me. My inability to follow simple instructions and my distinct lack of strength had brought a lot of attention in my direction. It wasn't the type of attention you want. There was also the fact that I was a member of the RAAF and across the whole of the Australian Defence Force, the RAAF is known as the soft service who eat ham sandwiches and wipe their fragile arses with three-ply toilet paper.

Face down and ashamed, the instructor's psychological tactics were starting to work and I found myself doubting my own ability. I then thought, 'If I can just get through this first day, I can get through the whole course.'

I got through the first day and the second and the third. Days came and went as they do, however, I remember this particular day. It was a timed 20-kilometre forced march with full kit. I had regained a lot of my strength, but not enough for this march. In lead-up training, I had completed similar marches well under time, however, this one, the only one that mattered, I didn't just fail, I didn't even finish. 'This is you done, Troy,' I said to myself, dejected and devastated.

I thought I would be thrown off course immediately, however, because special operation units only seek mentally strong, decisive recruits able to back themselves, selection directing staff (DS) don't provide any performance feedback or weekly counselling and there certainly isn't any hand-holding. Those of us that failed the march were pulled aside and told to go back to our tents, get some food into us and informed that we would be removed from the course, sometime in the next few days.

They attributed this delay in removal to the need to process the paperwork from us having failed a gated activity and offered a discharge on request (DOR) in order to expedite the removal. Most of the candidates completed the DOR form on the spot, but I smelled a rat. 'Surely, if they want us gone, we would be gone, I thought, making eye contact with the other two candidates that hadn't completed the DOR. 'Stuff it, let's stay,' I suggested under my breath.

Fortunately, my sense of smell is rather good and hence, my decision was vindicated. The three of us were allowed a retest of the march and all three of us passed, allowing us to continue with the testing of our physical and mental limits.

Despite eating mud and being owned, there were many enjoyable activities from selection. The ergonomic sled was one such activity. Some twisted soul had created these devil-like creatures. Picture, if you will, a large truck tyre filled with weights because a standard truck tyre is not heavy enough, right? Attached to this weighted truck tyre is a coppers log to drag said item up the Singleton roads.

The purpose of this horrific invention is for a five-man team to drag the tyre demon around Singleton's training area at 0100 hours in the morning, for a few hours. The catch is the coppers log is only long enough to fit four men carrying pack, webbing and a weapon.

Number five is carrying two water-filled jerries. Personally, I preferred the log. Now, I'm realising the actual intention of this activity was to break our backs or our souls, or both.

Towards the latter part of the course, the activities in the early hours of the morning were increasingly pleasurable. We had to stargate the building with sandbags. For those who do not know what a stargate is, it's a portal device that stems from the 90s TV series *Stargate*. It allows rapid travel between two distant locations, however fun stargating was with sandbags, it was nothing on my very favourite activity. This activity was conducted on the food and sleep-deprivation course. Yay, no food! Yay, no sleep! It just got better and better.

In order to stay awake, we carried out the Commando carousel. A carousel is a merry-go-round, but we had no pony to ride. We just ran around in circles like headless chickens on fire, following the red cyalume light stick from the candidate in front, for hours on end. Best ride I have ever been on. Highly recommended and if I could, I would give it five stars on Trip Advisor.

I'm sure you know I was being facetious when I used the word pleasurable in this chapter on commando selection. Coffee drinking is pleasurable, making love is pleasurable, listening to music is pleasurable. Selection is not. It is tough, but after having worked and deployed with multiple Special Forces units from here in Australia and around the world, I completely understand why they carry-out such activities during selection.

Some such activities involved water and one of the funniest moments from selection was watching British royal marines not being able to swim, during our water activities.

During the course, your rest is so important that you come up with ways to shave time off menial tasks. Mine was putting on my camo shirt. They were the old button-up shirts. Whilst I have no doubt, we were not the first, me and a few other candidates figured if we left the buttons' bar done up, we could just slide it on like a t-shirt.

Well, let's just say this one time that did not really go to plan for me when called up in the middle of the night to undertake some tasks. In my haste and sleep-deprived state, I managed to put my shirt on backwards. I had no idea until I presented to the directing staff, where it was ever so gracefully pointed out and ridiculed.

Talking about sleep, who needs that? Completely overrated if you ask me. I mean, despite putting on my shirt backwards, I still somehow managed to tie my boots after no sleep in God knows how long. By the final day of selection, I wasn't even sure where I was, until it dawned on me that I had completed a Special Forces Selection course. An overwhelming sense of elation flooded me and I slept for a solid 24 hours, not even making a dent in the slept debt I was owed.

CCT boys post selection. In the early days many crossed over to 2nd Commando Regiment due to CCT's teething problems.

The next two days dragged on forever, though I had completed the course, I hadn't necessarily passed it. They needed to collate all the information, scores and psychological evaluations gathered during the course, to determine if we had passed or not.

During these two days, waiting while undertaking mundane tasks, I had resigned myself to just having finished the course, a rare feat in itself and something to be immensely proud of.

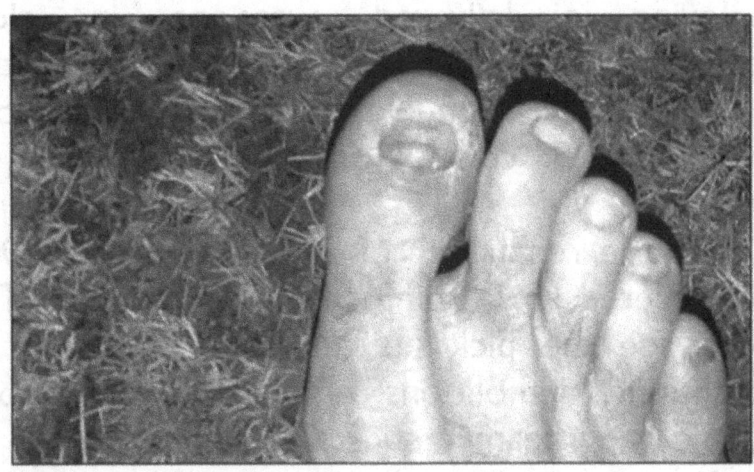

Foot post selection. I was missing multiple toe nails and the sole of my foot fell off.

By the time my selection course was finished, a second CCT had been deployed with the next 2nd Commando rotation and we were all proud of what was being called the red-headed stepchild. 2nd Commando Regiment was asking for more CCTs on each new rotation and when I arrived back at RAAF Williamtown, the CCTs from the previous selection were already working with the units PC-9/A(F) aircraft for their deployment. Having forward air controllers (FACs), with their own aircraft always at hand in the unit, allowed us to train realistically and hard. Forward air controllers are the airborne intermediaries between ground troops and anything that flies which carries weapons. Their facilitation of close air support (CAS) has a legacy that stretches back to the Korean War and they are instrumental in preventing fratricide when employing air-delivered weapons in close proximity to friendlies. They taught us to do that job from the ground; a skill now called joint terminal attack control or otherwise known as JTAC.

For the remainder of 2008 and during 2009, I completed my reinforcement training. This would see me pick up the necessary skills of parachuting, demolitions, amphibious operations, CQB, driving, team tactics and roping.

As combat controllers, we would complete the reinforcement training and then finish off with our air force (blue) courses known as our pipeline of JTAC, including weather observation, landing/drop zone survey and assault zone controller. It was two years of training and the fun had just begun.

In 2009, due to the success of the early rotations and the now evident viability of their capacity, the special tactics project was amalgamated with the forward air control development unit to form 4 Squadron Royal Australian Air Force. 4SQN, which is still active and is at the very forefront of land/air integration, to this day. During my time there, I had the pleasure of working with some of the best COs I have ever served under and along with a number of other inspiring operators, that insatiable appetite of ours would be filled with combat deployments.

## 12

# Fuck it, We Are Going Live!

'Unload, inspect and hang weapons,' I heard over my heavy breathing.

I was in the multimillion-dollar state-of-the-art room floor combat range (RFCR). The range is designed to train operators on how to move through a multi-level house, with multiple teams while shooting live rounds. I had just completed my last lot of training in pairs and my heart was racing as I knew what was coming next.

'Fuck it, we are going live,' called the grey-haired course instructor otherwise known as the Silver Fox.

'Shit's about to get real,' I thought as we were bumped up to team-level entries.

I would be lying if I said I wasn't feeling the pressure. I was part of the first group of three combat controllers to attend this advance close quarter battle course. The direct-action continuum was my first real taste of gunfighting courses and would be followed up by close quarter fighting (hand to hand combat) and an urban operations course.

You would think I wouldn't be nervous about going live because, by this stage, I had already been jumping out of planes, blowing in doors and, in actual fact, blowing up most things we could get our hands on. I had been driving fast and bashing cars around, fast-roping and rappelling through windows and even driving boats on the open ocean at break speeds.

All of the above was fun, to a degree. The reality of taking part in such potentially dangerous training is this, during parachuting we had three major leg breaks, all resulting in surgery, which halted the forward progression of the guys on the course. It took two of them an extra two years to finish training and the other guy was so badly injured, the Army found him not medically fit for duty and discharged him. I personally got knocked out and broke my back during parachuting. I witnessed guys nearly blow themselves up using explosives and I saw people fall from fast ropes. Being on the water was not all fun and games either. A tactical transit from over the horizon is boring and people often get seasick.

During my roping course, I decided to run my mouth (it's a problem I have).

'Bet I can make it from the top and into the window in one bound,' I told the instructor.

Knowing that from the top to the entry point of the window would normally be two and a half bounds, the instructor looked at me and laughed, 'Go for it.'

I lowered myself over the edge and with an almighty push-off, I let my rope open and descended like buggery. As I approached the entry point, I slowly tightened my rope, bringing me towards the window. I flew through the window, sliding along the ground on my arse before crashing into some furniture, much to the amusement of another instructor who was standing in the room for safety reasons.

I got off my grazed arse and ran back to the window so the instructor and other boys could see I was still in one piece. 'Not bad, ey!' I called to them with a big smile on my face, pleased at my own capability.

My shit-eating grin was soon wiped when I did not receive the standing ovation I had expected. Instead, I received a punch on the arm from a mate.

'What was that for?' I questioned him, rubbing my arm.

'You're a dickhead and now as a punishment for you showing off, we all have to attempt it,' he replied.

'Damn, I cannot win with them,' I thought, shaking my head. This taught me a lesson. Something that is good does not need to seek attention. It knows it is good and that is good enough.

The first part of the close quarter battle (CQB) course started with the usual briefs to trainees and the expectation and failure management policy, however, this time there was a twist. We were off to medical to have our blood taken. We were informed that, as many rounds are expelled while on the course, it was not uncommon to have elevated levels of lead in your system. We were also informed that, at the end of the course, blood would once again be taken and it would be matched against the base levels to measure any indicated change.

'What the?' I thought, 'how much shooting are we doing here?'

Before you are let loose in the range, you have to learn to shoot. And by shoot, I mean really shoot. You learn trigger manipulation, barrel control, speedy magazine changes and smooth efficient transfers between your primary weapon, whether it be the Heckler and Koch MP5 or M4, to your secondary USP 9mm pistol. Training starts slow at snail's pace.

'Forget everything you think you know,' an instructor told us. 'We are going to reteach you and teach you with positive repetitions to get rid of any incorrect techniques or habits that may have been created.'

The shooting began on a flat range, shooting at close ranges and then slowly increasing the distance. It became obvious that everyone's shooting was improving. It was now time. It was time for the first test of the course. It was time for validation.

Learning to run our guns. Excellent instruction by out 2nd CDO supervisors.

Validation was a series of timed, close quarter battle-style shoots using both the MP5 and USP 9-mm pistol. Once you add time to a test, the amount of pressure changes. Apart from being a timed test, the instructors also throw in a gas mask. The reason for having to wear the mask during the shoot is because in most hostage rescue situations, the operators use gas.

During the initial validation shoot, I only used my iron sights on the MP5 which, with the gas mask on, is a painful process. I dropped a few shots but still achieved the required score needed to move onto my second validation shoot. The second shoot I found much easier as I was using the aimpoint sight. As I had passed that, I was moving onto the next phase, room floor combat. I was, and I still am, a shit shot, so I must have had Lady Luck on my side during these shoots. Others were not so lucky and were removed from the course, for not meeting the required standard.

Everything is taught systematically and methodically. Room floor combat is all about learning how to work with each other and engage threats rapidly while on the move in confined spaces. It is unquestionably an art of its own.

A CCT assaulting up the stairs ready to make entry.

As the course progressed, guys were starting to fall by the wayside, with an increasing number of candidates being removed. People were receiving safety violations and subsequently it was bye-bye to them. Shooting outside of your arc of engagement and having your weapon cross over another person is referred to as lasing and is naturally a big no-no. As the pace and complexities of our exercises increased, so did the infractions. Lady Luck stayed by my side and I did not receive a safety violation.

This is where the course got fun. I say that with tongue in cheek. I was starting to fatigue due to the long days of shooting. The instructors began adding-in stair runs in full kit with gas masks on, just to add fatigue to our run-throughs. I was feeling both the mental and physical drain.

Being able to partake in an assault on aircraft made up for all the stair runs. The course finished with assaults on aircraft, trains and buses, which adds another level of complexity to engagements in confined spaces. I thought I was a freaking ninja on that aircraft.

I was one of the first combat controllers to complete the course, and I'm proud to say that. Following that course, I undertook the close quarter fighting component of the continuation package. This was a short course of wrestling and jujitsu, but it revolved around doing it in full body armour. I was not much into wrestling, but there was something kind of fun about body-slamming someone while wearing full body armour.

I later did a stint with the tactical assault group (TAG) for the 2014 Commonwealth Heads of Government Meeting in Brisbane. While on a training course where we were rescuing hostages from a building, I had a role-player get a little too enthusiastic and he overplayed his role.

Trying to create his own scene, he grabbed my weapon. It was an absolute pleasure to put the training to use, I had completed years before. Throwing him to the ground, I performed a rock and roll wrestling-style body flop onto him before calling for assistance and cuffing him.

***

As the scout of the team, I had been moving down the side of the village. I moved past the open door, clearing most of the room by pieing it as I went. Pieing is a term for doing a sweeping arc across a doorway while moving past it, weapon up at the ready to engage any would-be threats. By doing this, you clear three quarters of the room without having to enter.

I looked at my opposition across from me, nodding to indicate I was about to make entry. Aggressively moving through the doorway, I instantly assessed a threat, a mock-up enemy. With three to five rounds, I dispatched the would-be threat.

'Good, Knighty,' came a voice from behind. 'Next time, try and add a little more movement while you engage. Remember, a moving target is harder to hit.'

I smiled to myself, thinking how I was enjoying this urban operations component. We had been shooting out of cars, over cars and in and around all kinds of protection you would find in an urban street. Weeks prior, I had been on a flat range, learning new skills and now I was applying them in the 'Afghan village'.

Apart from the fancy-pants, high-end multi-storey building, the 2nd Commando Regiment had a purpose-designed, specially built Afghan village. I would find out later it definitely looked and even smelt like the real deal. We had been moving through the village applying the tactics, techniques and procedures that operators on previous rotations had learnt.

Throwing hand grenades into rooms, shooting over vehicles and engaging from ladders were all now a common part of my day, no different to having a shower and putting on my underwear.

The final mission profile was planned from start to finish, with team leaders from the regiment who had been in actual contacts in Afghanistan. I was in awe of this level of training and it was by far the best I had experienced on a reinforcement training course.

After passing the direct-action contingent, I undertook a few more specialist courses before completing my reo. I then went onto my Air Force suite of specialist courses. Funnily enough, most of my instructors turned out to be team leaders and team 2ICs from the company I was first attached to for my special operations task group (SOTG) rotation. The Punishers from Delta Commando company being such people.

Continuous training is important, it doesn't matter who you are. Before the direct-action contingent, I thought I knew stuff. Turned out I knew jack shit. This is something I've now taken into my civilian life. You can never stop learning. You never rise to the occasion but will always fall back to the highest level of training.

Vehicle assault to the stronghold. Something kind of fun hanging off the back of vehicles.

Breaching training.

# 13

# Walking the Blue Pipeline

Pulling out my inclinometer, I measured the angle of the tree, or as we know it in the aircraft world, the controlling obstacle. This particular measurement would determine the threshold or touchdown point of the aircraft.

Six months before, I was dropping bombs and kissing mums, as the saying goes. I was a CCT filling the role of the JTAC for my Special Operations Task Group rotation. I was shooting and getting shot at, but now I was on the survey course and it was boring as batshit. I mean, an inclinometer? That name alone sounds like something out of Nerdsville.

The survey course was supposed to be something new, an exciting challenge for me. A course which was run by Sergeant G and had a US training team, teaching us the arts of surveying an airfield. Our US brethren had been landing aircraft on deserts, wastelands, highways and random pieces of properties for decades and I could learn a lot from them.

I quickly realised that I was not that interested in survey. I just wanted to shoot weapons and drop bombs. This course, however, was important for me to move forward into a true combat control unit instead of the Special Operations JTAC I had become.

'Righteo, Knighty, you have the angle, now calculate the threshold for your Australian C-130,' yelled VW, the American training team instructor.

'Schoolwork never ends,' I thought. 'Piss off and annoy someone else.' Truth is, VW and his counterpart Sully were aces in all things survey. They pioneered and set the standard for the US. They had landed the A-10 Warthog on highways, for God's sake.

I had thought that roaming around on a piece of dirt was boring, but then, I entered the classroom. Lessons on trigonometry and Pythagoras theory came flying my way and I had nowhere to hide. Another ageing controller, by the name of Geoffro, was in the classroom with me. We would look at each other, knowing this was going way above our heads.

Apparently, sines, cosines and tangents are simple, but not for his little black duck who didn't pay attention in his senior high school years. To add to this unruly issue, the flight lieutenant entered the classroom. He had a big head and an even bigger brain. You definitely wouldn't lend him your hat, because his head size would destroy it. He and his Mensa-level analogy tried to reteach us not only about triangles, angles, rise over run, but he also started talking about this ancient Greek philosopher who knew all types of shit about maths. My head was seriously hurting and I just wanted to shoot something.

My self-discipline kicked in and after a night of laborious study, I passed the test the next day and completed my initial assessment of an airfield using minimal tools. 'Just land the plane,' I thought to myself.

Then came, the Penetrator. Yes, that's what we called it, but its actual name is the dynamic cone penetrator. It is an advanced piece of equipment and the single most important piece of equipment for landing an aircraft.

In engineering terms, this device measures the soil-shearing strength. To dumb it down to my level, the device, along with a few other calculations, tells the combat controller how heavy an aircraft can be and how many moves we can use for that piece of dirt.

As the survey skill set progressed, so did the technology. Nowadays, survey is completed in a third of the time, thanks to an Android phone and some brilliant mind who created an application. The app not only looks after the survey but also the dropping of bombs. Kids these days don't know how easy they have it.

As part of the progression, the unit began utilising an independent third-party consultant STS Inc., otherwise known as special tactic solutions. Their instructors are retired 24th STS combat controllers. under Joint Special Operations Command (JSOC) who specialised in Assault Zone Operations, Desert Landing Sites and

Airfield Surveys. Their real-world experiences range from operations conducted in Saudi Arabia, Kuwait, Somalia, Bosnia-Herzegovina, Afghanistan, Iraq and many other locations throughout the globe, including an Emergency Action Plan and surveying for US Embassies and Diplomatic Facilities worldwide. Each instructor has brought a vast amount of experience and skills to the course.

'A long way from being just a JTAC,' I thought to myself.

We sought these guys out because we wanted the premier former unit guys to train us. That was the direction the Australian Combat Control Team was headed and still is now.

\*\*\*

The joint terminal attack controller course was four weeks long when I completed it back in 2009. I had used that skill set to drop bombs in Afghanistan in support of my Commando brothers. I believe that, due to increased requirement under the US-Australia Memorandum of Understanding, it is now six weeks in duration.

The course starts at a relatively slow pace, learning about radios, general patter and requirements we need to transmit to the aircraft. Although it starts at a slow pace, it does not stay that way for long.

When I completed the course, it was predominantly run by pilots and former fast-jet guys. Anyone who has anything to do with the pilot stream in the Air Force can attest to their overachieving ways. When you are on a pilots course, it is sink or swim on a daily basis. The way they ran the course was no different.

During my course, we used the slower moving PC-9 and now the PC-21, which is organic to 4SQN, the Hawks and the F-18 Hornet. The F-18 would come flying in at roughly nine nautical miles per minute, so, as you can imagine, if I was assessing the jet's geometry towards a target, there is a lot of pressure and not a lot of time.

In saying this, most of the guys get through without much trouble as the unit screens quite aggressively. Prior to a gruelling physical selection course, combat controllers are screened with a battery of tests, both for IQ and EQ (Emotional Intelligence). These tests are run out of the University of Newcastle. Again, part of picking a smarter human.

A number of my stories in this book revolve around the dropping of bombs. I'm not going to bore you with the specifics of the JTAC course, but I will say what you do on the course is a completely different beast to dropping bombs in combat and there are some situations that you just can't train for.

\*\*\*

If my suite of blue courses seems piecemeal, it is because it was. I originally was just a Special Operations JTAC. We all were. If it was not for the forward thinking of the earlier guys, we would not have had combat control. Instead, we would have stayed within the JTAC role only. The capability became what it is today because of guys like Sergeant G, who single-handedly wrote a paper and put forward a foreign military sales case to have a training team from the US teach us survey. We had two flight lieutenants design the air-traffic control package for us, or as we refer to it as assault zone control. If it was not for the forward thinking of these guys, I have no doubt that CCT would not be where it is today.

\*\*\*

'Fuck me,' I said under my breath as I entered the classroom. I had just returned from my close quarters battle course and had been on a high from gunfighting and running through the house to now talking about lows. We also talked about highs and fronts as we pored over charts. I was on the weather course.

'This is going to be the worst,' I thought to myself. I mean, weather is what everyone talks about when they have nothing else to talk about.

Turned out I was wrong. The aviation weather course is a certified course through the Bureau of Meteorology. I found the prediction and observation of weather quite interesting. I have since used this learned knowledge to support my hobbies such as parachuting and shooting. I use my skills to help keep myself and others safe, predicting surf and winds for my surfing, skydiving and base jumping.

So, it turns out I'm a bit of a weather nerd, go figure. I impress all types of people with my weather-reading abilities. Thanks, ADF, best course ever!

Assault zone control wasn't the best course ever, but it did have the coolest course title, and it was the last of my courses. This course teaches the candidate how to run an airfield in an austere environment. It takes into account the operation of an airfield in a conflict or kinetic situation, something an Australian air traffic controller cannot do. Deconflicting helicopters, fixed wing aircraft and a bunch of ground troops who have no idea about aircraft procedures. Sometimes, these situations can be like herding cats.

CCT landing an Australian C-130 on an Austere strip.

\*\*\*

'What's the future of Combat Control in Australia, Troy?' I often get asked.

Like everything, the job constantly evolves. It has already been dynamic in its movement, spreading into a different spectrum of operations. The new guys are pushing the boundaries in ways akin to the older guys and the older guys are still pushing the boundaries, themselves.

At a time, which I liken to post-Vietnam, the days of kinetic operations are over. At least for the time being. The Australian CCT, with the guidance and training from their US brethren, have already planned and trained for that next contingency.

I see women being a larger part of the CCT. As I mentioned, it is not all about kinetic operations. I worked with some outstanding women in my bodyguard work.

I often refer to CCT as its own entity, but it is more than that. It belongs to 4SQN Royal Australian Air Force. None of combat control's work would be possible without the organic support of the unit, such as the clerks, the logistics staff and the pilots. On average, it takes roughly five support staff to get one controller out the door and it's obvious that the success of Australian combat control would definitely not have been possible without the combined efforts of 4SQN staff.

# 14

# Red Dust Beginnings

*Alone at Dawn* is of one of my favourite books. It's a true story written about the series of events which lead to a US Combat Controller John Chapman receiving the Medal of Honour. Written by Dan Schilling and Lori Chapman Longfritz, the book also discusses the US Combat Control team history. The co-author Lori was John Chapman's sister. John Chapman was a career US CCT member left behind on Roberts Ridge by his own Navy SEAL Team. John was the first CCT member awarded a Medal of Honour for single-handedly assaulting multiple gun emplacements on his own.

*Alone at Dawn* discusses, in depth, John Chapman's heroic acts, which ultimately saved the lives of the rescue force and the problems/frustrations of the US CCT in its beginnings. It's funny how history repeats itself and us modern Aussie CCT would find ourselves facing the same problems.

In the early days, we were effectively just Special Operations Joint Terminal Attack Controllers. We kind of reverse-engineered it from our US brethren. The Yanks ran landing zones, drop zones and surveyed airfields first and it was always the vision of the early Aussie controllers to mimic the skill sets of their US counterparts, given their strong experience in the CCT space.

One of the issues for the CCT is that no one is sure how our capability even came about. Rumour has it that at a mess function, the Special Operations Commander told the Air Commander that it couldn't be done. Bets were laid and off we went. Is there truth in that story? I really don't know, but no one else has a better one.

The capability also faced the problem of recruiting airmen and officers prior to having any real infrastructure and logistics involved. I mean, who would want to join a unit with no support?

We did, however, know where we wanted the unit to go but just not how. Thankfully, some determined airmen and officers put their heads together and planned a way to commence this task and make it happen. As luck would have it, the Okinawa-based 320th Special Tactics Squadron planned a training activity and reached out to see if we wanted to send any controllers. Sergeant G and Sergeant S were chosen to go, as the activity was going to be survey-based and they had the biggest passion for it. They were headed for the Northern Territory. Hello, red dust!

There was lots of enthusiasm but limited funding. The boys managed to get themselves to the Northern Territory for the activity, only to be greeted with no accommodation or hire cars.

These logistics should have been booked by support staff but weren't. Underprepared was an understatement! They had limited personal kit, no survey equipment and even little things like GPS were scarce. They were, however, resourceful enough and managed to sort the issues for the most part. When you don't have a hire car and the only car available is an old XD Falcon you take what you can get. This vehicle was an 80s-era station wagon, not the best car to be driving on the rugged Northern Territory roads with their fine powdery talcum-like dust. Of course, the boys ended up covered in said dust, just in time to meet their immaculately presented US counterparts for the very first time

Inroads were starting to be made and the initiative was gaining traction. The exercise had been a success and both Sergeant G and Sergeant S had really grown their knowledge base. Professional, positive relationships were formed and suddenly, there were emails back and forth from the US Combat Control school house.

Combined U.S & AUS training activity. Without the involvement in the early days of U.S CCT, the capability would not be where it is today.

A gentleman by the name of Mike Anderson paid a visit from the US and presented us with various ways to solve the issues we were facing. The favourite option was to source funding from the US Department of Defence foreign military sales program. The foreign military sales program facilitates sales of US arms, defence equipment, defence services and military training to foreign governments, and it also sources trainers from the US CCT survey shop. The survey shop houses all the gurus and knowledgeable instructors in the area of survey for the US CCT.

The FMS was approved after the writing of a series of papers on capability with varying courses of action and recommendations by

Sergeant G. The US Government was paying for our training and they released a training team to fly to Australia to teach us. It had been an absolutely outstanding effort made by Sergeant G to make this happen and get the capability off the ground. This rate of effort and initiative taken by Sergeant G was later awarded with a Conspicuous Service Cross.

CCT Conducting a survey of a landing zone.

In late 2010, a two-man US survey team came over to Australia to instruct the unit. They brought with them equipment and their vast knowledge of surveying runways and drop zones. As I was deployed to Afghanistan at this time, I missed out on this very well-run course.

I got my chance on a survey course the following year. There was, however, still one big problem. No equipment, or a distinct lack of it. Trying to get funding released for top of the range equipment, for a new unit no one knew anything about, was hard to say the least.

Providing taxi instructions to a C-130 Hercules.

'That's it!' snapped Flight Lieutenant S and off he went on a mission to buy equipment. He had given up on the funding and believed in the unit, so he used his own money to buy some much-needed but very expensive equipment. The following course, he and I were on together and I have to say, this equipment certainly came in handy. The mobile training team from the US kept coming over with all their spangle-dangle equipment and kept running informative courses. Overall, the Aussie survey capability was starting to take shape and a strong alliance with our US counterparts had grown.

# 15

# Fuckery and 500-Pounders

It was a balmy summer's evening and I was pondering if, one day, I might actually become more careful in what I wished for. I was about to be inserted into a cluster of villages called Gonbad in Shah Wali Kot, Afghanistan.

No coalition troops had patrolled in Gonbad for six years and it was renowned as a Taliban R & R stronghold. This was at the forefront of my mind as I sat on the tarmac, double and then triple-checking my radios and weapons while awaiting the helicopters. This was my first job with 2nd Commando and I was determined not to fuck it up and let the boys down, especially as they had welcomed me so generously into their close-knit circle.

\*\*\*

I sat still and silent in the dark, waiting for the dust to settle to see if our insertion had been compromised. While I had been on board the UH-60 Black Hawk, I was maxing out with adrenaline and anticipation. The pucker factor had only increased as I stepped off and away from the relative safety of the helicopter and into the Afghan dawn.

The job was a standard clearance and search mission, with the further goal of gathering intelligence on any high value targets (HVTs) in the area. We were only carrying enough food, water and ammunition for the planned 24-hour duration of the mission.

As the dust settled, I saw that our position was secure, however, it didn't take long for my bum cheeks to pucker back up, as the enemy quickly made its presence known, attacking another call sign in our company-sized force.

'Contact!' blasted through my headset.

Uncharacteristically, the company was engaged in our first contact of the tour, trading small-arms fire with several Taliban spotters who were quickly dispatched. Periodic rolling gunfights ensued but don't get me wrong, it wasn't Custer's Last Stand by any means.

My team's task was to provide an overwatch of the clearance with our Afghan partner force. It was the teams in the clearance element that were the troops in contact. Multiple friendly positions were reporting taking fire over my radio, while I tried to manoeuvre a Heron unmanned aerial vehicle (UAV) overhead, to get sensors on the enemy. Amongst the gunfights, there were periods of absolute stillness and, as the sun rose over the land, I consolidated my overwatch position to truly provide support if things really kicked off.

The sun had risen and lingered high and hot in the sky when, abruptly, my consolidation and deliberation were broken with a 'troops in contact!' call over the net. A numerically superior Taliban force was overrunning one of our teams. The Talibs, always crafty as hell, had snuck up and ambushed them. The team managed to break contact but in doing so, they had left behind some valuable equipment. The boss wanted to get the precious equipment back, so he ordered me to get some CAS to sort out the problem.

Another JTAC, known as MS who had a better vantage, accepted my offer to work as a team for the bomb drop. I focused on battle-tracking the friendly call sign, while MS briefed the arriving CAS pilots, taking them to the enemy location.

I won't lie, battle-tracking a team who is fighting for their lives in a close combat situation, while I have minimal time to report on their rapidly changing position, is indeed a little tricky. It is, however, absolutely necessary when high explosive bombs are involved. I had a job to do, and it had to be done to the absolute best of my ability, regardless of my situation.

Once any ambiguity had been removed about everyone's exact locations and MS received authorisation from the powers that be, they calmly transmitted 'Cleared hot,' and with that, the enemy were no more.

Now, that story makes me sound like I did a great job and all the Commando boys would be proud of me, but I neglected to tell you that while the team were in contact, I stood up, thus, drawing fire to our position. 'WTF, Troy? Are you a complete idiot? I mean, even an untrained civilian would be unlikely to stand up in plain sight of the enemy!'

I am an idiot. I do stupid things. I will put it down to a lack of morning coffee and the fact I was fixated on locating the other team that so desperately needed help. In an effort to locate the friendlies, I stood up, peering into the distance through my laser rangefinder. Naturally, we immediately came under fire with splinters of shale kicking up all around and the unique *crack hiss* of supersonic projectiles barely missing us, ringing in our ears. I was so focused on the task at hand that I didn't get the memo and in hindsight, I like to think that I must have appeared to all present, as Robert Duvall's Colonel Kilgore in that classic *Apocalypse Now* 'Charlie don't surf' scene.

Perhaps not a classic movie fan, one of our assaulters KJ crash tackled me to the ground, querying me as we fell, 'What are you doing you RAFFie fuckwit? Don't you know we are being shot at?'

It's difficult to explain the bond formed between brothers during a contact. Though I was green and stupid, I can sleep at night knowing why I stood up, however, I have forever resigned myself to being introduced as, 'This is Troy, the stupid RAFFie that stood up in a gunfight with no cover.'

Sitting in overwatch after getting the shit shot out of us.

All fuckery aside, MS did manage to neutralise the enemy, freeing the team to return and secure their previously discarded equipment, consolidate with the rest of the company and have a snooze. A little sleep could always be enjoyed between 1100 hours and 1300hours, because that's when the Taliban take a siesta. As all of Afghanistan fell peacefully quiet, we met them halfway, pausing our clearance and finding a shady spot for a well-earned break.

Too soon, heralding the end of the lazy ceasefire, the Taliban aggressively opened fire on our multiple positions with large-calibre weapons, laying down accurate fire on the clearance teams. My request for close air support quickly arrived and my jets soon checked in.

I had achieved the best observation point and had developed the highest situational awareness of the enemy position, so I took control of the aircrew. With a racing heart, I plotted the enemy position on my map. I was about to drop my first bomb in anger and a lot closer to friendlies than is ever allowed in training. To get any of the time-honoured regimental process wrong now, could kill my mates or myself.

With as much courage as I could muster, I passed on the enemy coordinates to the aircrew who punched the coordinates into their onboard systems. That information then fed to a bulging, 500-pound, GPS-guided bomb slung under the wing, waiting hungrily for its target.

With the jet inbound for the attack and all checks complete, the rubber hit the road.

'Cleared hot,' I transmitted.

'One away,' was the calm reply in my headset.

'You, beauty,' I thought, 'my first release.' Still, I was shitting myself, hoping like all hell that I had provided the correct data to the aircrew because with a GPS bomb, once it's 'off the rails' as they say, 'you bought it,' and nothing could stop it now on its inexorable flight to its destination.

The bomb made a loud whistling noise as it rent the air and *schwacked* the target. A direct hit and high fives all round, right? Well, not quite. The thing went low order with only the meekest of explosions compared to the organ-jarring thump I had sought.

The first bomb I dropped. Yep, the one that did not detonate.

The Taliban, undeterred and presumably laughing at me under their *shemaghs*, were still engaging the teams. I quickly instigated a re-attack on the same target with the original jet, a procedure that allowed me to significantly truncate the process while still meeting my legal obligations.

'Faaark,' I cursed the sky gods while having a tantrum fit for a two year old who wasn't getting their lolly. The second attack had been a carbon copy of the first. A direct hit, however, another low-order bomb.

Sensing, perhaps, that they may not be so lucky a third time, the Taliban did cease their engagement. This hadn't been the JTAC baptism by fire I had imagined, but it had effectively met the boss's intent, which, in the final analysis, is the total sum of my job.

With no other attacks required, I checked the jets off, having learnt a very valuable lesson, two is one and one is none. From then on, I always tried to throw down two bombs at a time.

The Afghan sun was settling and we were preparing for our extraction when word came through from headquarters that theatre and strategic assets were receiving a lot of useful intelligence from our mission. We were asked to remain in location for another 24 hours. Checking our supplies, we agreed, knowing that we could stretch them out, however, we knew we would soon be getting hungry.

After day two in Gonbad, the head shed had realised that they had stirred up a hornet's nest and so, ordered a further extension to our mission. All supplies were low and we were hungry and I don't do hungry very well. We had already started redistributing ammunition and, of course, food and water were in short supply. In our job, the highest priorities are mission-essential items like ammunition and radio batteries. Then comes water and, finally, food.

I wouldn't want to test it, but there's a rule of thumb that states that one can live for three days without water and three weeks without food. Fortunately, a resupply of provisions came that night to carry us over the next period of darkness.

The following morning saw a lull in contacts throughout the valley. Suspicious, I directed an MQ-1 Predator UAV overhead and spotted some armed Taliban on the high ground behind us, manoeuvring into assault. I called for close air support and a pair of A-10s, with call sign Hawg checking in. This gave me an instant gratification as A-10s are the JTACs' wet dream and their aircrew are masters of close air support.

The wet dream team quickly located the target, recommending engagement with 2.75-inch rockets and 30-millimetre strath. Clearing them hot, I watched as the jets made short work of the threat before departing, to save the day elsewhere and make another JTAC wet his pants. I was elated, having neutralised the enemy for the boss in a seamless application of JTAC procedure, thanks to the professionalism of the Hawg crew.

That afternoon, a cloud of dust rolled in, to try to extinguish my elation at a job well done. This was one big dust storm, lasting two days, much to our dismay. The choking dust penetrated the *shemaghs* we used to cover our nose and mouth. Visibility was significantly reduced, so much so that the helicopters, to be used for our extraction, were unable to fly. We battened down the hatches, preparing for our third night in Gonbad, as the storm raged.

Dawn, on the fourth day, saw a muted orange sun shimmer, as it wavered meekly in the east. With the dust still whirling, we were blind from above as the MQ-1's cameras were unable to penetrate the storm, and the Taliban knew it.

Engagement from the enemy started immediately. Some of this fire was originating from the site of the first target location, where the bombs had failed. Because I had already confirmed data for that point, I could put down another GPS bomb without aircrew needing to sight the target, effectively relegating them to the role of airborne artillery.

Convincing the boss that close air support was the go, I requested some jets. You can imagine my surprise when a B-1B Lancer bomber called me from somewhere up in the stratosphere!

'What am I going to do with a strategic bomber?' I asked myself quietly. The aircrew checked in with more weapons than Australia had in its entire inventory and so I briefed them to deliver three 500-pounders for a simultaneous impact on the target.

Inbound and cleared hot, the aircrew declared the weapons away and so I waited. And waited and waited. Due to the altitude of the bomber, those bombs fell for a lifetime.

I was shaken from my reverie by an almighty explosion as a volcano of molten shrapnel erupted skywards. All bombs impacted exactly as planned and detonated, completely flattening the enemy position and curtailing any fire from that position for the rest of the mission.

What 3 x 500lbs bombs look like to neutralise a Taliban ambush.

During the day, gunfights did continue from other positions, however, didn't meet the threshold for close air support. The dust storm had been relentless and by evening, had got worse with visibility down to near zero. We remained stuck in the middle of that shit storm, unable to be extracted. We were low on ammunition, radio batteries, water and food.

Due to the heat, the clearance teams had resorted to drinking from the local water source, a risky proposition at the best of times, as it was also used as a toilet by the locals. A night extraction was very much preferred, due to the threat caused by enemy small arms and particularly, rocket-propelled grenades, a weapon that could easily down a helicopter. However, due to the dire situation of our supplies, the US airlift component in support was on standby ready to extract us, as soon as the weather cleared. Unfortunately, that fourth night passed with no hope of a safe extraction.

As the crimson sun rose, we had been in location for five days with only enough food and water for two. We were nearly out of ammunition and only had one working radio left, when a call came through sounding like the voice of God himself. God said, 'Exfill to the LZ.'

At the landing zone, we huddled behind rocks for some sort of cover when my radio suddenly sprang back to life, with an American voice at the other end. Another pair of A-10s had arrived to protect the airlift element and they were flying at an extremely low level, so as to remain in sight of the ground, the dust storm only having marginally abated.

I briefed them on the friendly force disposition and established that both were FACs. I delegated authority to them for weapons release, requiring that they contact me before any attacks so I could quantify the risk to friendlies. Hungry, tired and just plain spent, I was concerned that I might make a fatal mistake in my fatigued state, so it was a relief to have such competent pilots overhead. The FACs also offered to coordinate with the airlift element, so all I had to do was kick back behind my rock, listen in on the air radio and mark the landing zone when the helicopters arrived.

'Extraction inbound, five minutes out,' came the call from my new A-10 buddies.

My distinct preference was to mark the landing zone with a smoke grenade but for fear of alerting the enemy to our location, the boss requested I use a VS-17 marker panel, a metre-square piece of fluoro-orange cloth, carried by JTACs to signal aircraft.

Breaking cover, I moved to the centre of the landing zone, removing the cloth from my pack and unfolding it. Holding the cloth out in front of me, like some lairy matador goading bulls, I awaited the helicopter's arrival.

The lead CH-47 Chinook materialised from the gloom, charging directly over my head. The second bird tried to land on me. Luckily, I was blown clear by the downwash of its two massive rotors, so I wasn't crushed by the giant chook. Unfortunately, the sixty or so kilograms of gear I was carrying knocked me unconscious, driving my head into the rocky ground.

I came to, finding that the first CH-47 had already departed and the second had its ramp up with its engines spooling, ready for take-off. The senior team leader MT, who was on the first helicopter, realised he was one man down. Advising the pilots, they radioed the second aircraft, advising it not to leave without me. The second aircraft's engines powered down and you've never seen anyone get off their dusty arse and leg it as fast as I did. You can only imagine my relief, as on my approach, the crew lowered the ramp and helped me aboard.

Due to the delayed extraction, the Taliban had emerged from hiding and were attempting to engage the helicopters while the A-10s lit them up all around. 'Well done, Troy. You've done it, again,' I thought to myself, slumping into a webbing seat as the helicopter took off and returned us safely to Tarin Kowt.

That first combat mission had truly been one of both fuckery and 500-pounders and one that taught me some very valuable lessons. Lessons such as how, if you don't rise to the occasion, you just fall back on your level of training. Or how to recognise when I was maxed out and losing situational awareness. These would be valuable lessons that I would take with me in future missions, however, that first hit out as a Special Operations Air Force combat controller had almost been a complete clusterfuck. I mean, I stood up in the open during a gunfight, dropped bombs that were duds and nearly got left behind! Sterling work, indeed, for someone helping to build up a new defence capability.

# 16

# Luck of the Irish, but I'm not Irish

Halfway through my first rotation to Afghanistan, the Taliban really started to ramp-up their use of Improvised Explosive Devices (IEDs) in the province of Uruzgan. These nasty devices, though primitive in design, were highly effective and both the local civilian population and our colleagues in the mentoring task force (MTF) had felt the brunt of this change in tactics.

My platoon was tasked with a kill/capture mission, hunting a particular IED-maker in the western reaches of the province. Closely situated to where our intelligence reports had indicated this terrorist's location was, there was an Australian forward operating base (FOB). The team leaders and the boss created a plan to push multiple teams out to the FOB using our well-armoured Bushmaster infantry fighting vehicles. The mission would be staged from the base.

Getting to the base required a slow, hours-long night move with the use of night vision goggles (NVG). The move was uneventful as we successfully avoided a number of IED choke points. We entered the base and set up a staging area in one corner. While the boss and team leaders discussed with the MTF guys their thoughts on the location of the high value individual (HVI), I busied myself with establishing a Heron overhead the nearby towns. The Heron started scanning the compounds below with its sensor, establishing a pattern of life and seeking the bombmaker.

Geared up and ready to go, the team was waiting on my sensor feed to show signs of the terrorist, however, the feed had nothing. Sourcing alternative human intelligence, the boss gave the thumbs-up for the mission to proceed.

'You, beauty,' I thought to myself, but then I saw the boss make a beeline in my direction.

'Knighty, you will be staying behind. I need you to stay here and work the Heron from a static position,' the boss ordered me.

I immediately got the sulks, but I knew he was right. The Heron UAV I was working, had a shit communications system and really needed to be worked from a static position for it to be rendered effective.

I was pissed off. I wanted to be out there with the boys but no, I was left in the rear with all the gear. I know I'm not the Lone Ranger when I say that I just wished our masters might occasionally consult with end users, before spending millions of dollars on dubious equipment.

Still sulking like a child, I set-up a game plan with the boss.

'Boss, I will keep the Heron's sensor locked on the compounds so you can see what's going on. If there's contact, I want to go out, though.'

The boss seemed to agree as I highlighted how having the Heron's sensor locked on the compounds would improve his situational awareness.

The teams advanced on the compounds making multiple breaches, but finding nothing inside. The compounds were dry holes. Obviously disappointed, the teams returned to the base. I was secretly not disappointed. I was quite happy that I hadn't missed out on anything, short of a physical training session with some heavy kit.

'Knighty, wake up, wake up,' the task force soldier said to me as he cautiously shook me awake from my shut-eye. It was midday and the usual heat was evident on my clothing as I woke in a sweat.

'You need to ring the lead JTAC back at home base in Tarin Kowt,' he informed me.

I got straight up and straight on the blower. The lead JTAC, known as SD, was excited. He told me that he was pushing for a MC-12 intelligence, reconnaissance and surveillance (ISR) aircraft, as the HVI had been positively identified near our location.

The operators geared up, the boss and team leaders worked on a plan. I geared up too, as there was no way I was missing out on this one! This was not going to be just another PT session, that much I knew.

The MC-12 was equipped with a much better communications system than the Heron, allowing use by the operator while on the move. This meant I would not be stuck in the corner. No one sticks Baby in the corner. Okay, no one sticks Knighty in the corner.

The sensor operator had managed to correlate the HVI to the same series of compounds that we had previously breached and her feed confirmed the expected pattern of life, aligning with the indications we were confirming on the ground. 'Let's get this fucker,' I thought to myself.

The teams stepped off, eager and ready to roll. It was a speedy and stealthy infill to the target, taking into consideration that we were in broad daylight, from a location with an extensive Taliban spotter network.

We entered the lush, habitable areas located near watercourses known as the Greenbelt. The Greenbelt is just that, green. An oasis amongst the otherwise avid and harsh landscape of Afghanistan.

Closing in on the compounds, we began our search. Watching the feed, I hadn't seen anything from the compounds, so all indications were that the HVI was still in that location, however, he wasn't to be found.

'Where was the fucker?' we asked ourselves. After a period of head scratching, and I will note here that it wasn't from lice, despite the relaxed grooming, the decision was made to once again exfill back to the base.

The teams consolidated and moved off, leaving the Greenbelt and proceeding into the expanse of desert surrounding the Greenbelt known as the *dasht*. Suddenly, we were at the receiving end of some small-arms fire. The rounds seemed to be directed to the team at my rear. Being the last man in my team, I pulled back a little in support, drawing fire as I went.

I received a target indication from one of the rear team members and observed movement coming from the left of the area of engagement. Then I saw them, two enemy fighters moving to a new position. I must have let rip about ten rounds and not one of them hit them. I had missed completely!

'You shit shot,' swearing at myself under my breath. My teeth were clenched and I was pissed off at myself, however, I realised I had a primary role to play and that was as the platoon JTAC.

With haste, I jumped on the radio and established contact. The sensor operator had watched the whole thing unfold on her screen and surmising that I might have had my hands full, she had searched for and pinpointed the threat. In keeping with the rules of engagement (ROE), she provided the coordinates of multiple, fleeing enemy and confirmed their hostile status.

Within seconds of me receiving this information, a couple of teams were in pursuit of the fleeing enemy. I was providing the information from the aircraft above, however, the ISR eventually lost the enemy as they had fled into thick shrub with large overhead trees. The hunt was called off, without us coming back with the quarry.

During the pursuit, I had pulled a map from my pants pockets. The map had a little hole in its corner, but being task-focused, I didn't think anything of it. Now, the team had returned and were consolidated. It was then I noticed another curious little hole in the same side of my pants pocket that my map lived in.

One of the more senior operators noticed the bemused look on my face. He looked at the hole, then at me and spoke, 'That's a bullet hole, mate. You've been shot.'

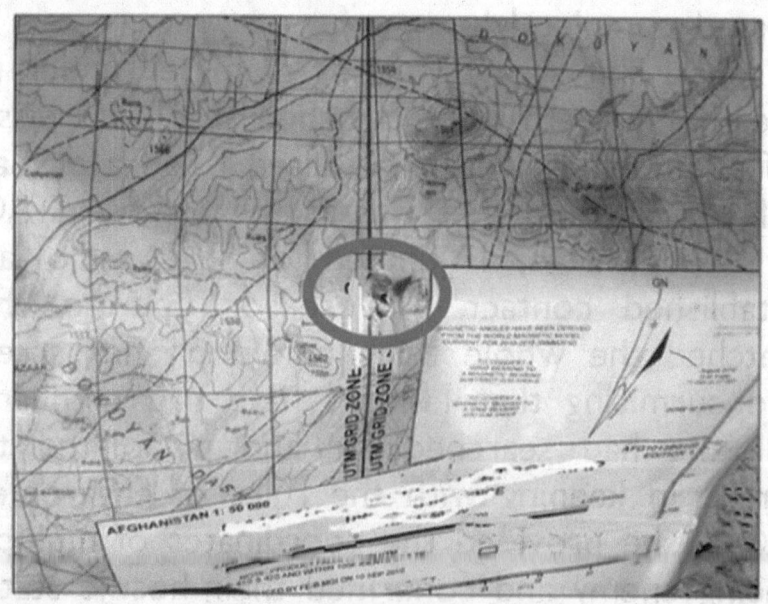

The hole in my map.

The boys, with their total lack of empathy, started winding me up, 'Ha ha, the RAAFie's been shot,' they laughed.

Me, with my bullet hole and no other injury to prove my gallantry, recommenced the exfill with the teams.

*Boom,* the sound of a large explosion rang out from the Greenbelt. I saw a plume of grey smoke billowing from the tree line. Someone had stepped on an IED and it wasn't us. Unscathed, we safely made our way back to the base.

Back at the base, a forensic examination of my pants ensued. It was determined that the hole had most certainly been caused by a round.

'You are bloody lucky, Knighty, to have been wearing those baggy cams,' one of the operators said to me.

I nodded my head in agreement, thinking how I was fortunate not to have worn my tighter cams. Now this (and a million other reasons) is why I refuse to wear skinny jeans.

Post mission showing off the hole in my pocket.

The following day, I found out that the target had blown himself up. That explosion we had heard was him disseminating himself with his own device. That device was meant for us, but instead he reaped the outcome of his own work. He was known as an expert bomb-maker, but clearly, he wasn't as good as everyone thought. So, this is why kids, you don't play with bombs.

# 17

# Dzangal

'What a cracker this job is going to be,' I thought to myself, walking out of the secure area where I had been part of a topsecret discussion with a fellow US combat controller. It was going to be a joint operation with the US Special Forces.

Our job was simple. Fly into a valley that connects the Helmand province to Uruzgan and stir up a shit fight. The US Special Forces with their Afghani partner force would come in behind to clean-up our excrement.

The area we were about to stir up was a known ratline or movement area for Taliban commanders moving to and from Helmand province from the relative safety of Uruzgan. Intelligence had suggested there were several Taliban commanders in the area, enjoying some relaxation time. Unbeknown to the vacationers, FE-Bravo and their US Special Forces counterparts were about to add some excitement to their holiday.

Crammed into our planning room, the boss, team commanders and myself, pored over the map, spitballing ideas on how to achieve the mission. My part was simple. I just needed to come up with an air asset and sensor plan, then put in a request for air assets, and that was my job done.

I did, however, need to know the plan or scheme of manoeuvre. By understanding where the teams were and, of course, where the most likely threats were, I could prioritise the sensors or bombs from the supporting aircraft.

It was decided that I should go onto target early with the snipers for this job. I would have a prime overwatch position and going in early would build my situational awareness.

'A trained monkey can pull the trigger,' I had once heard a sniper say to an assaulter. There was always a healthy rivalry between the assaulters and the snipers. They each thought they were better than the other and slandering was not uncommon.

'War dodger,' the assaulter would say to the sniper, referring to how they sit and hide away from the action.

'Dumb bullet catcher,' the sniper would reply.

I had not been out on a job with the snipers before, despite knowing them all. The snipers did tend to be the more experienced operators and I felt a level of anxiousness fall over me. 'Switch on, Troy,' I said to myself. Sergeant AM, the sniper team leader, grabbed me. AM was a down-to-earth, no bullshit kind of guy. He spoke to me in a cool, calm and collected way, which reassured me of my skills and the need for me to be on his team for the mission.

Once AM had given me back some confidence, he asked lots of questions pertaining to the air assets and how they could be supported? I do, however, suspect he already knew the answers, as he had worked with a former combat controller who had transferred over to the 2nd Commando Regiment and was now a sniper.

After my pep talk, I joined the sniper team in their own planning office, where there was an array of satellite imagery and various other mappings spread out over the desk. The team was looking for suitable hide-out locations and places to occupy in support of the assaulters in the Greenbelt.

Cover? What is that? Scanning the mapping and imagery, we could find no suitable areas with cover. The Afghan high ground is a mixture of rocky outcrops and bare earth. The only location we found semi suitable looked to be an old Russian fighting position from the 1980s.

'That is going to be IED central,' chirped one of the boys, pointing at the map. Everyone nodded in agreement. Without further discussion, it was decided that the team was adding an engineer from Special Operations. These guys had balls of steel. I mean, who the hell actively looks for bombs and then disarms them? They say I have a screw loose, but I look completely sane next to them.

\*\*\*

Ahh, nothing like the smell of Avgas to make you feel like you are alive. I caught that familiar whiff and the sound of rotors turning as I walked towards the Black Hawk. We had the US premier helicopter unit in support for this mission and as it was a mission to stir up the proverbial hornet's nest and then shit in it, it was decided to land on, or in our case, land somewhat close to, our occupation site.

Waiting for insertion into Dzangal. My heart was always racing and I was constantly visualising scenarios through my head.

Landing about three kilometres from our occupation site, we disembarked our helicopter. After a period of sitting and listening on the outskirts of the village, we began our short but steep walk to our overwatch position.

Leading the way was our engineer with a sniper on his shoulder for protection. The engineer was waving his magic wand, a device that resembled a souped-up version of a metal detector. The movement was slow and laborious, but it kept us alive and with all body parts intact.

We arrived at our hide, with the engineer clearing the area. I use the term hide loosely, as this old Russian fighting position was just bare ground, basically an overt overwatch. I'd had an MQ-1 Predator covering us the whole way. Even though we landed close, there had been no local national or Taliban activity. 'A good sign,' I thought to myself.

***

'Ten miles,' squawked over the radio as the rising of the crimson Afghan sun began to break the skyline. It was the assault force-led helicopter giving me the heads-up that they were inbound. It had been an uneventful night and I had the MQ-1 searching the land zones for the helicopters. 'LZ's cold,' was the call and all aircraft were inbound with the assaulters.

Upon landing, the assaulters hit their predesignated compounds. The signals specialist piped up, 'Hey AM, there is a significant increase in icom chatter since H-hour.'

All indications pointed towards the opposite mountains. The valley ran north to south and had mountain ranges on both the eastern and western side. I was on the western side and the enemy appeared to be directly opposite me.

Pushing the AH-64 Apache helicopters towards the area, within minutes they had identified two armed individuals scurrying into the rocks. The Taliban were far from stupid. They knew the AH-64s would bring the hate with their 30-mm cannon.

With the boss's blessing, I began to engage with the attack helicopters whose pilots I all knew by name. I'd had a few engagements with them previously and we trusted each other. We had a dedicated lift and attack helicopter support in Tarin Kowt, from the US.

30-mm and 2.75-inch rockets rained down on the enemy and they ran, then hiding in a small cave. I do not blame them, I would have too. Escaping the attack helicopters was essential for their survival.

The fluidity of warfare still amazes me. One minute it is peaceful and the next, utter pandemonium. The operators of the regiment excelled at this. With a sudden change in plans, followed by a quick coordination on the radio, I was suppressing the enemy with the AH-64 Apache. A Commando assault team was working their way up a near vertical cliff face, their mission, to close with and kill the enemy.

It was on from the morning. I had to suppress this hill whilst operators from the 2 CDO Regt assaulted up the cliff face towards a Taliban fighting position.

Sitting in the comfy, albeit, exposed overwatch position I was in awe of my mate Murray's team assault up this cliff face. 'Stuff that,' I suddenly thought, as Murray's team was getting close to the objective and had eyes on the cave.

'Cease engagement,' I called through to the AH-64. I kept the helicopters low and overhead to keep the Taliban's heads down. The noise alone, was enough to stop the Taliban engaging.

'Frag out,' came the call. One of the operators tossed the US-made M67 grenade into the cave. We used the US grenades because they actually killed people. The Aussie-made and issued F1 grenades were shit. Multiple times we had used them and they did not achieve their objective. The Australian grenades would land next to people and detonate but with no effect.

Making entry into the cave ensured an exchange of fire and the assaulters quickly dispatched the assailants.

'Two enemy killed in action,' came the call over the radio. The helicopters were on minimal fuel and had to return and all my nasty air-power weapons had returned for home. The only aircraft I had was Australia's unmanned Heron.

Due to planning commitments and controlling of aircraft, anyone designated in the Joint Terminal Attack Controller role barely slept. This meant I had only minimal sleep in the past 48 hours and I was now feeling it. I tasked Heron with a sensor taking-in the support of the assaulters hitting the compounds of interest.

'Get some shut-eye,' sniper team leader, Sergeant AM, directed me. The assaulters in the Greenbelt had been in minor skirmishes throughout the day and we were certainly achieving our task to stir up the proverbial, but AM could see I was spent. 'We will go 50/50 stand to. Put your radio on speaker and I will wake you if needed,' he continued.

I fell asleep and dreamed. I dreamt nice dreams. Dreams of surfing and feeling the water on my body and the connection with the ocean that only a surfer knows. I was world's away from the Kush of Afghanistan.

'Get out of here, we are getting hit!' AM yelled at me, whacking me in the chest. I awoke groggy and confused. 'What the hell is going on?' I asked myself.

As my eyes started to focus, I saw the dust kick up around me. This sight made my senses and will to live immediately kick in, and I realised what was going on. I was being shot at, again. AM had grabbed his gear and already taken a bound back, laying down covering fire into the area the fire was coming from.

I applied a lesson learnt from those who served in Vietnam. Throughout our training, we were constantly taught to have only minimal equipment out, to achieve the task. This was one of those times where it came into practice.

I had slept in my body armour and had my weapon by my side. Also, beside me, was my pack, inside it was the old school, heavy, ground-to-air radio with an attached satellite antenna. This was a necessary evil in order to talk to Heron.

It was like something out of *The Matrix* as my satcom antenna took a round from an enemy combatant and it was instantly slung metres behind me.

'Move,' came the call from AM.

Myself and the sniper TL running for it after having my SATCOM antenna shot.

'I am out of here,' I thought, as I grabbed my pack in one arm, ditching my satcom antenna. I legged it and moved past AM, yelling, 'On me'. This was a call to insinuate hasty movement without fire to a designated area. I had spied a low piece of dirt which provided protection from fire. My patch of dirt was already occupied by a couple of other snipers and a medic, who had been shot out of their overt positions by the enemy. 'Not a bad spot for a reunion tour,' I thought, as I slid into position like I was sliding into home base.

'Hell for anyone who disturbs my sleep,' I thought angrily to myself. 'These guys are going to pay.' With that line of thought, I immediately jumped on the radio and requested some air support.

The boss kiboshed it straight away. 'Negative, ANZAC,' came the call. 'We have this.' ANZAC was my call sign for this tour.

'But, boss,' I complained, 'These fuckers not only shot at me, but wrecked my sleep.' As petty as it sounds, sleep is precious.

In the ditch after getting the shit shot out of us. We copped more rounds since Matty decided to be a smart arse and stick his head up. Radio in hand begging the boss for air support.

With no air support and not being able to return fire, the five of us sat in this depression till nightfall. No wonder they call the medical condition depression, because this depression was depressing. For me, it was a bittersweet moment. I never liked getting shot at without returning the hate, but the boss was correct in not letting me flatten the place because my precious beauty sleep had been abruptly interrupted. He had sensed that I was pissed off and may have made an emotional mistake. Now, that is good leadership.

Night fell into a welcome silence with the darkness, and with it came the subsidence of enemy fire. We were due to extract and exchange with American Special Forces. We had achieved our mission of shit-stirring it up.

'When are these helos coming?' I asked myself. I was tired and all emotional from the operation. Like a teenager who has had their mobile phone taken off them, I was still stewing over not being able to engage with aircraft after being shot out of my position.

I was so moody I may well have been that teenager because I had drawn the short straw. Extraction would see me in the rotor wash seat. It was a pinnacle extraction, meaning the helicopter landed on the mountain we were on and we were replaced by a US overwatch team.

The position of the back right, with open doors on a Black Hawk, is without a doubt, the worst position to sit. Also, I was stropped in. Let me tell you that being stropped in is not all that it is cracked up to be. It involves cold air, no back support and in my case a major case of rotor wash.

'Just great,' the moody me thought, as I copped a beating with rotor wash.

Following the rotor-wash beating, landing and then debriefing, I moved towards the mess. I needed food. The food helped to change my attitude back to normal, as did the conversation I had with my commander. It was a very adult conversation and this ever-so-intelligent man explained his reasoning for no air support. This was, however, after he and the team commanders had apparently laughed their arses off, at the sight of me running like crazy for cover. Apparently, the snipers breaking contact made for good morale. I could only smile.

# 18

# Vegas, Baby!

It was 2011 and I had just returned from my first Special Operations tour to Afghanistan. It wasn't a boring tour and I had experienced my fair share of engagements using my rifle and also aircraft. I was allowed a short R & R break over the Christmas period, some unwinding time to spend with my children and wife who I had not seen me for five months. I tried to unwind but found myself thinking only of work. I don't think I really made the effort I should have with my family, while on my return from deployment, but I didn't see it like that back then. It was all about me.

Given my world had slowly started to rotate only around myself and my wants, you can imagine my excitement when I found out I was going to the US to work on a combined joint activity with US and British forces. This activity was a massive training exercise using all types of aircraft. In my opinion, the training just can't be replicated over here in Australia. It was to be my first multinational training activity and I was pumped! My elation skyrocketed to a height that went beyond over the moon when the training location was disclosed. Las Vegas, baby! Yep, 'Viva Las Vegas'. I can inform you that my wife did not share in my elation. The look on her face was one of disdain.

'What? Six weeks in Las Vegas on a holiday?' she questioned.

'No, babe,' I replied. 'It's for work,' with a wry smirk on face.

'Bullshit,' she said, as she walked off, unimpressed and undoubtedly visualising her husband throwing money onto gambling tables and drinking all sorts of alcoholic concoctions.

I spent the next couple of weeks in the proverbial doghouse. This time at home was meant to be a special time to share with my wife and family, but it wasn't turning out that way. I told her not to worry about me being in Vegas, as I would probably be stuck out on a range somewhere, because the ranges are out of town at the Nevada test training site, home of the infamous Area 51. I don't know if my lying skills were starting to deteriorate or if the length of time I had spent away was getting to her, but she still wasn't buying it.

It's not uncommon for military personnel to be away from home. We had already spent two years apart at the start of my training, with my wife and I only seeing each other a couple of times a year. This separation didn't bother me, I was loving the job and the deployments. Too caught up in my own rockstar tours, to realise what was happening to my marriage.

Before departing for Las Vegas, we undertook some intensive lead-up training. This training included long-range shooting, CQB shooting with the guys from 2nd Commando regiment and of course, our bread and butter, working with aircraft. During this lead-up training, time flew by quicker than one of our fighter jets. I had worked hard and I was feeling satisfied with my skills. The last thing I wanted was to be the Aussie that would embarrass themselves in front of the US and British Special Operations guys.

My dedication to the job must not have gone unnoticed as I was chosen to head over on the advanced party. 'Another win,' I thought to myself, as this meant I would be in Las Vegas even earlier than expected.

I travelled with the unit's senior airman and the boss, for that trip. There were many other Air Force personnel joining us and we definitely were not the main event. My feeling of being super special had been humbled. While in flight, it felt peaceful and mystical flying in and over the mountains around Nevada. The hilly terrain I could see excited me. I liked to climb and run trails and I was hoping I would get some time off to explore the region.

Once we were on the ground, the group of us picked up our hire cars and the lead officer directed us to where we were staying. There was one problem, the hire car company had run out of GPS navigation systems. With this information, a few smart people in the group bought data cards for their phones and used them, so they knew where they needed to go. Was I one of the smart ones? Nope, I am dumb and a tight-arse and so I decided to wing it with a comical looking tourist map. 'What could go wrong?' I thought to myself. 'Here I am in a brand-new city, driving on the wrong side of the road and driving a car that resembled a monster truck. Piece of piss.'

I was notorious for dodging driving duties and once again, I managed to dodge this one and I was relegated to the back seat. Of course, without a GPS, this journey was not a piece of piss. It involved a series of wrong turns, driving into oncoming traffic and generally getting lost. By some miracle, we made it to our destination. I think it must have been my smart-arse comments and generally unwelcome advice that got us there safely.

'Holy shit, we are staying at a casino! You, beauty!' My level of elation was now at a level, equivalent to that of a child visiting a combined puppy dog, fireworks and candy store.

We checked into our rooms and freshened up, ready to reconvene with the rest of the party. The room wasn't luxurious nor was it a daggy themed room. Dressed more like a standard hotel room, the suite was equipped with everything we needed. I was sharing the room with the senior airman of the party. He was a good bloke, however, I was happy the room had two queen-size beds.

Once we had reconvened, we were told that we were to have a day's rest, as is the policy after international training. 'Yes, Sir,' I thought myself. I wasn't going to argue about having a day off in Las Vegas. The team were starving, so we went in search of food. The needed sustenance was found in the form of a burger joint inside the casino. I was on a low-carb diet, with the exception of beer. Given my dietary requirements, the waiter recommended that I try the turkey burger. In this particular burger, the usual buns are replaced with chunks of crisp iceberg lettuce. Ironically, this healthy burger was loaded with fatty cheese and I couldn't get the beer in fast enough. I have to say though, this burger is the very best burger I've ever consumed and gets the Troy Knight five-star rating.

Like a pack of ravenous lions, we quickly devoured the food. Most people in the military eat quickly. You learn to do that pretty much from day one at recruit training. Eat quickly or miss out. I know I wanted my dinner done, so I could step out into the blinding lights of Vegas. My first point of exploration was what is known as The Strip.

'Holy shit,' I said quietly under my voice.

'What was that?' one of the lads asked.

'Nothing, 'I quickly replied. 'It's just this place, it's amazing.'

I wasn't lying. I was actually blown away by the sights in front of me and surrounding me.

There was so much to take in, almost a sensory overload of flashing lights, colours, fancy casinos and beautiful people. Everything was massive. Massive lights, massive casinos, massive cars and people with massive hair.

There were people with big hair everywhere. I will describe it like being in a theme park crossed with a nightclub. I saw the sign for the *Coyote Ugly* Bar. 'Oh, this is going to be good,' I thought to myself.

I wasn't wrong. It wasn't just good. It was very good. Actually, it was better than very good. It was awesome. The bar looked identical to the movie named after it. Behind the bars and often dancing on top of them, were a number of staff members. They were professionals and could mix any drink you wanted and certainly put on a show, making the punters stay for more drinks and bar dancing. I was one of the bar dancers. I had an alcoholic shot literally shot down my throat with a Super Soaker by one of the waitresses. As soon as you start dancing on top of anything, you know you are already gone and your only intention is to party.

Did I party? Of course, I did. Did I pay for it the next day? That's definitely affirmative. I awoke to a massive hangover and I had lost my wallet and identification. On the plus side, I was in my own hotel room, with all my teeth still in my mouth and not a tiger or baby in sight. One smart decision I had made the night before was that as my form of identification I had my driver's licence and not my passport on me.

'Good one, Troy, great start,' I said to myself when I realised what I had lost on the first night. The boys gave me shit for being so irresponsible, but I could barely hear them through the banging of what was my own heavy head. I spent most of the day just trying to rest and rehydrate, so I would be in some type of operational form. I couldn't get away with any malingering on this trip!

By the next day, our training equipment still hadn't arrived as it was due along with the main party, in a few days' time. This, however, didn't mean we sat around twiddling our thumbs. There was always plenty for us to do. On the base, we attended lectures and safety briefings, and there were all sorts of logistics and meetings with key personnel. A huge amount of time and effort goes into making these large-scale international exercises work.

The Nevada Test Range was a nightmare to get into. It was the highest security I've ever encountered. The paperwork side of it was insane. I regard myself as being quite privileged to have been there, as I believe that, nowadays, they don't let any non-US Citizens enter. There were of course no-go areas where we could not go. These areas were fenced off and there were also roads we could not travel along.

The urban range and the air weapons high explosive (HE) ranges were our training ground.

They had real tanks, armour and other aircraft for us to bomb. The Americans really do go all out. Completely unreal. The urban range is an actual city so you naturally do not drop live HE on that, but it's used for what we referred to as dry CAS. In this style of exercise, we go through the procedures and calls with the aircraft releasing the weapon. This type of training is priceless.

I knew the training was going to be good and my excitement level grew as the team started to talk out scenarios and plan serials. This type of planning is important because when using aircraft, you want to have your training objectives sorted, otherwise you are flying around a multimillion-dollar government asset for no good reason.

K was the senior airman in charge of running the training scenarios. I was not qualified at this level to run such courses, however, due to my active imagination, he asked me to help create some scenarios. I willingly accepted this request and the clockwork inside my brain started ticking.

By the time the main body arrived, the advance party was already in full swing. We were organising base and range passes and generally planning the whole scenario. With the full contingent now in Las Vegas, we sat down and were given a serious talk. The kind of talk you give to a teenager about not drinking at a party just because others are doing it. The talk was designed to fearmonger us out of partying and just generally being out. We were informed of the mugging culture, what to do if you are pulled over by police (so they don't shoot you) and where to avoid, at all costs. There was a casino called The Palms which was on this extensive list. The Palms was known for gang-related violence. Just like a defiant group of teenagers, the first port of call for that night was The Palms Casino. All I can say is that I'm still alive.

Our hot Vegas days consisted of meeting the aircrew and working out their training objectives. These exercises generally run themselves due to the support and infrastructure, however, you can plan specifically for your own training. The team found out we would be working with the A-10 Warthog Squadron, the British Tornado Squadron, an MQ 9 Reaper Squadron and the Australian C-130s for some airfield/airdrop work. Breaking down into teams helped with the training and created a rotational system for all the range, which was much needed for a combat control training activity of this size.

We got on with the exercise activities and I could not get enough. This was the shit I had signed up for. This is what I lived for. Shooting, moving and communicating. I was in my element.

By far, the exercise in the urban village was my favourite. The exercise pays privately owned US companies to play the enemy. These companies had professionals, their own equipment and were using Hollywood-style makeovers to make them look like enemy from certain countries. They were even using pyrotechnics worthy of a *Die Hard* movie to make explosions and fake rocket propelled grenades fly through the air. Americans, you got to love them. I mean, how could you not love them when one of them had their own C-130 with enemy paratroopers that jumped out onto us? Impressive, to say the least. I had quickly worked out two things about the U.S. These were 'go big or go home' and 'more is more'.

Following one of our training activities, the boss devised a brilliant plan. The plan was to show off the capability of the newly appointed Air Force combat controllers, as they were not getting much traction and to be honest, a large part of the Air Force didn't know what this new capability was even meant to be doing.

The Air Commander was in town for a visit to witness how the exercise was working out. The boss informed us of the plan. The plan was to invite him out to demonstrate our capabilities, but this plan was a little different than the standard plan.

'Lads, we are going to have it that the Air Commander is a tandem passenger on a military freefall from an Australian Air Force C-130. He will meet us on the ground where we will have a scenario built for us to fight through the city.'

I had a big grin on my face. 'Genius,' I thought to myself as the boss continued to explain his plan right out of *Wile E. Coyote*.

The plan had all the Hollywood mastery put into it by the security company playing the enemy. We put everything into it too, and hence, the exercise was executed at a very high level. The Air Commander landed safely after a perfect landing by the tandem master. What was happening was explained to him and I can remember a big grin spreading across his face and us being ordered 'fight's on'!

Fight on we did with simulation rounds whizzing around leaving paint marks and large bruises on anyone that had been hit. The fight through the town consisted of big explosions, fake IEDs and fake RPGs. Close air support was on station and the A-10s were working their arses off at low altitudes for us. There were buildings simulated as being hit with the pyrotechnics. Part of the scene had one of the boys getting blown up by an IED.

I had recently completed the first aid course. The course is designed to upskill one of the team with a high level of medical skills. Now, I got my chance to put my training into action. I attended to one of the casualties. He was in bad shape and required me to apply training tourniquets and start a cannulation on him to replace some of his fluids. I got the Air Commander to assist so he could witness my newly acquired skills. Now, I will admit that running an IV and cannulation to start fluids was something I was not so great at and of course, I stuffed it up. A vein rolled on me and there was not enough time to start another one. Pulling a swiftie, I instead taped it up as if I had completed the procedure and ran the rest of the usual checks. The fact was that I didn't even turn the bag on.

'Did you just put an IV in?' the star-ranking officer asked me.

'Sir, I did. Just one of the many skills of a CCT,' I replied.

I was quite happy with myself for pulling one over the big boss and I still am.

As the scenario played out, I was impressed by the Air Commander. He really kept his cool despite all the explosions and battle activity. I thought he would have been maxing out with adrenaline and losing situation awareness, but no, he was cool, calm and collected. The man absolutely kept his head in the right space. In hindsight, I shouldn't have been surprised as he had been a fighter pilot flying around at 540 knots and pulling crazy Gs. This officer was trained to deal with sensory overloads.

There was a big smile on his face at the end of the scene. The debriefing supported his smile as he was thoroughly impressed. My boss, added to the debrief, mentioning about getting better equipment and support. Well, I can tell you his wish was granted. The cashola started rolling in to buy equipment. This was also the start of a long friendship with the man who is Chief of the Air Force and would be my pick for Chief of the Defence Force.

\*\*\*

A fastball was thrown at us, we were to be at the range immediately. To save time, we got kitted-up in our equipment on the base where we were. It was a mixed training activity with 2nd Commando Regiment, so the vehicle passengers consisted of operators and combat controllers. The drive was only short, but we were running late so we thought a little extra speed would not hurt. I mean, we were driving on the interstate. No one would notice us. We did notice the sirens and lights.

'Shit,' we all said in unison.

The situation is this. Six armed guys crammed into a tiny vehicle, with a seventh guy thrown in for good measure. As the highway patrol officer approached, we obeyed all the procedures that we had been taught. The officer approached from a dead spot where we could not see him as he closed in. The hand of the approaching officer was on his pistol. 'Good drills,' I thought to myself, 'he doesn't take his job lightly.' He reminded me of one of the characters from the old 80s TV series *Chips*. I was about to say something smart to him, but for once, my brain actually worked and I kept my mouth shut. 'Well done, Troy. You are learning,' I thought to myself. The cop didn't shoot us and actually was a really good bloke. A former serviceman himself, he let us explain our story in full. He then let us off with a warning to keep our speed down and also took the time to thank us for our service. 'Well, fuck me dead,' I thought. 'Maybe I should have joked with him about looking like Eric Estrada from *Chips?*'

For the remaining five minutes of our trip, we were escorted by the cop, now known as Eric. I will sell it as an escort, however, it was more like Eric was probably making sure the dodgy Aussies were telling the truth and not heading off to rob the local bank or something. Dodgy Aussies, dodgy as the proverbial.

For the remainder of the trip, there was pretty much an even amount of work and play. We worked hard, but to be honest, we probably played harder. I know I did and by the end of the trip, I was exhausted and ready to go home. Five weeks was way too long in a city that never sleeps for a guy who's most likely on the spectrum. Our team of Aussies were supposed to fly back on service air, however, the aircraft was re-tasked for a humanitarian disaster relief effort. It was not a bad deal for me as it meant I was going back by commercial air. 'You, beauty,' I thought to myself. I much preferred the comforts of commercial flights.

The flight home consisted of me catching-up on some much-needed sleep. Once landed and processed through the routine border clearances, I turned my phone on and it blew up. It consisted of a thousand missed calls and some very irate messages from the wife. 'Oh no,' I thought to myself, 'what's happened?' I was confused by all the messages and so I texted her to ask what all the fuss was about. Well, it turns out that me and a few of the other boys were in trouble for posing as male strippers from the Thunder From Down Under show and the wife had found out and she was not impressed with what was supposed to be a harmless joke. That little joke that the boys and I went along with caused me much grief, but hey, at least I didn't get married again. Vegas, baby!

# 19

# On a Wing and a Chook

'Oh fuck,' I thought to myself as I saw the light turn green. 'What the hell are you doing here, Troy?' My inner voice suddenly asked. 'I don't know, but it's too late now,' I answered back as I clenched my butt cheeks and threw myself out of the aircraft.

Up to that moment, the thought of jumping out of a perfectly good aircraft excited me. Because of this seemingly irrational thinking, the basic parachute course was part of the selection process that I was particularly looking forward to. It is a static line jump, meaning all you need to do is clip the line onto a fixed cable. The cable will deploy and hopefully open the parachute from the pack that is attached to your back. It all sounded like such a simple process, but as per usual, I was wrong.

There are so many factors at play in parachuting. The training is painful, intense and at times, mind-numbing. There are drills and mock-ups for all different scenarios. There are drills for when you are in the air and there are drills for landing. Due to the great height you are deployed from the aircraft, when making the jump and the speed you arrive on the earth, there is only one preferred method to land. Stuff that up and you are most likely looking at a spinal fracture or a fracture of one or both of your legs. I made sure I paid the utmost attention during these lessons as I had no intention of ending up in a wheelchair.

There were also emergency drills. What to do if you are going to hit a tree. What to do if you are going to hit wires and what to do if you are going to land in water. Lots of what Ifs. All these drills were repetitively fed into our skulls, but all I wanted to do was throw myself out of that aircraft.

That moment of self-questioning immediately turned into an absolutely thrilling one, as I felt my shoot open and the slight jolt to the body that it causes. It was such a rush and something that really only those that know, know. It was this first jump that got me hooked on jumping, whether it be in the military or as a civilian.

I was immediately an addict and I wanted to jump again, right then. Due to pure luck and weather holds, I managed to have three successful jumps before most of the other combat controllers had even had one. Not being able to hold my tongue, I let the lads know all about it. A fair bit of friendly banter, well mostly friendly, was going back and forth between the boys on the course. Naturally, after only three jumps I thought I was one of the sky gods and the lads should be worshiping my proverbial golden wings. Little did I know that irony can be a nasty bitch.

Parachutes have wind limits for a reason. It's to stop cocky and inexperienced jumpers like me from thinking they literally have wings.

After multiple weather holds, stopping us from undertaking jumps, I was pleased to see light winds and blue sky. I was going to get another jump and another one up on my mates. Due to some of the other lads, I was being made to wait. I hate having to wait my turn.

'Darn,' I thought. After waiting around all day, finally my turn to jump had come but so had the weather. The winds were up and close to the permissible limit.

'I want this jump,' I said to myself as I rigged up and boarded the plane. Once airborne, my heart sank. The team onboard was told that the winds were over the limit. The aircraft circled for what seemed like an eternity and I was praying to the wind gods to be kind. The wind gods didn't hear my prayer, because the winds kept up, but someone else must have heard it because the drop zone safety officer asked the Commanding Officer if we could waive the wind limit. The CO agreed. 'Beauty,' I thought, rubbing my hands together. 'We are in.'

This is where I fall from the pedestal that I had put myself on. Something or someone bigger than me was going to teach me a lesson.

I did not hit the ground running. I don't even remember hitting the ground. All I remember was the sky was littered with parachutes and upon opening, I had another paratrooper in my canopy.

The unwelcome visitor was descending at a quicker rate than me, and he couldn't help but steal my air. This was not a good position to be in, and I was coming in for a landing close to the sound barrier. 'Oh God,' I said to myself as I watched my pack hit the ground first.

***

'Knight, wake up!'

I awoke to the staff talking to me. At first, I had no idea what had happened. It took me a while to remember who I was, why I was there and what had just happened.

After some time, I came to. I was strapped onto the drop zone medical bike and taken off to be examined. The medical officers poked and prodded me, and an X-ray was undertaken of my C-spine, which is located at the top of your neck.

I was thankful that it all checked out fine. I didn't feel all fine, but I kept my mouth shut in fear of being removed from the reinforcement cycle.

Years and much back pain later, I went to a doctor and requested a complete spinal X-ray. The radiologist reported that I had had a previous compression fracture. This degeneration of the spine was shown to have happened at the same time as the parachute training, so this was then added to my military records.

The airborne gods must have thought I had learned my lesson as later in training, I managed to complete the military freefall course, unscathed. Well, just.

The initial jump you complete on freefall is a nine-stage series of jumps. These jumps are to the exact standard that the Australian Parachute Foundation run. In fact, many of the training instructors are the best civilian jumpers in Australia and subsequently, the world. This is very comforting as a student, knowing you are being trained by the best.

By this stage, I had already spent much of my own money on getting civilian jumps under my belt. The military may have this uncanny knack of being able to take the fun out of everything, but the flip side is not having to pay for the jumps. I rather liked jumping on the government's dime.

As I was now a qualified civilian jumper with over 500 jumps, I was fast-tracked through the system. As a safeguard, however, the fun police required me to go up for a stage nine hop and pop, which is when a jumper exits out of the aircraft, stabilises and releases the canopy.

I grabbed my canopy and proceeded with my checks. The instructor came over and introduced himself. We pre briefed the jump, talked about possible malfunctions and then dirt-dived the jump. A dirt dive is a practice run of the actual dive.

Following embarkation, the aircraft proceeded to the required height. I stood up and my instructor completed his checks on my equipment. Ready for deployment, we moved to the ramp and suddenly, the jump light was green. I backed off the ramp and felt the immediate rush that I was addicted to. I stabilised and deployed my canopy. 'So far, so good,' I thought to myself as I fell through the air.

I quickly orientated myself and under the canopy, I completed a series of turns and a brake check, to make sure there were no issues with the canopy's steerability. 'All good,' I said to myself. There is a feeling of elation about being under the canopy. I had a bird's eye view of the world and I felt at peace.

Returning to the drop zone, I glide across and through the air, making a series of turns cutting my altitude all the time, while doing my wind checks and making sure I didn't go downwind of the drop zone.

In parachuting, you run what is called a circuit. Remarkably similar to an actual aircraft. Hold upwind, turn downwind, base leg and finals. Downwind leg is when the wind is on your back which accelerates you. Base leg is a turn at right angles to your approach or finals.

I checked my altimeter and realised it was time for my downwind leg. Turning with the wind, I began my downwind run. I reached the point past the drop zone, where I estimated I should turn and commence base. There were no issues yet, however, I needed to keep my eyes on the prize. 'Keep concentrating,' Troy, my own self-preservation said.

Hitting my desired point, I pulled on my front riser for a 90-degree turn onto the finals. Coming in hot, I completed a quick situational awareness check to make sure I was clear of any other jumpers.

'All good,' I said as I came in, hitting my flare point and landing nice and soft.

Despite the fact I had performed this type of jump many times previously, I was on a course and I was also the first CCT and Air Force guy to be on said course. I wanted to perform well. I needed to perform well. I was happy with myself. I had performed well, or so I thought.

Walking over to me straight-faced, my instructor undertook the typical military debrief.

'How do you think you went?'

'Not bad,' I replied. It was true, I had executed a stable exit and I had decent canopy control.

'I concur 100 per cent,' my instructor replied. I could tell though, that there was something else. He continued, 'What was the assessment requirement?'

I answered with a series of answers, none of which was the correct one. Seemingly giving up on me after his prompts, the instructor stated, 'You landed next to the packing shed, where were you supposed to land?'

'Shit,' I thought to myself. I finally understood what he was getting at

'You are a student,' my instructor said, putting my head back onto the ground I had just landed upon. 'The requirement for you was to land out there, on the alpha.' The instructor pointed to the alpha which is the wind designator and aiming mark for the drop zone.

In the civilian world, if you hold a certain licence, most drop zones have an alternate landing area. Due to my own civilian experience, I was used to landing on an alternative drop zone and that instinct had taken over. I had, however, mucked that one up. 'Good one, Troy, way to bring attention to yourself,' I thought, shaking my head at my own ignorance.

'Grab a rig,' my instructor replied, smiling. 'We are going up again for your retest. This time land near the alpha.'

I did as I was told, grabbing a rig and just happy to be given the opportunity to do a retest and, of course, another jump. I jumped and everything went smoothly. I literally landed on the alpha. To be honest, I probably just dragged my foot across it, but at least it wasn't next to the packing shed!

Following this, I joined the trainee jumpmasters as a member of their stick. This role included checking the team jump gear, planning the jump and leading the jump in. I found this all very enjoyable but not as much fun as what I was about to undertake.

Combat equipment. Jumping combat equipment to be exact. Now, that's fun. Combat equipment (CE) is a combination of pack and webbing. Jumping CE changes the way you fly. You have to arch harder and you tend to slide backwards.

Exiting the aircraft with my pack. I was the first CCT to complete the military freefall course.

'I want you to become unstable and regain control,' my instructor informed me, prior to my final CE descent. I just looked at him with an odd look on my face. He must have read my face as he explained to me that his reasoning was that he wanted me to feel what it was like to experience that situation while in this environment, rather than at night-time under night vision with the team.

'Fair point,' I thought to myself.

As the aircraft climbed to height, I sat there with my eyes closed, with a visual rehearsal being performed in my mind. During this visualisation, I pictured myself exiting, stabilising, completing my required tumble, regaining control, altimeter check, ground check, horizon check, opening and canopy check. I spent more time on this visualisation than normal because I had never experienced being unstable with CE, and to be completely honest, I was shitting myself.

'Everybody wants military freefall until you are on a one-way trip to Cypress City,' a mate had said while on the ground. On land, I had been in deep conversation with some of the other lads who had already experienced being unstable with CE. The word terrifying, had been used a number of times and if the boys were trying to terrify me, they were doing a good job of it.

'Breathe, Troy, you have this,' my inner Zen-like voice told me softly, trying to ease my nerves. Back on the aircraft, I was given the usual time call and I went through the checks and moved to the ramp ready to be airborne. The light turned green and it was go time. I was off and I hard arched and stabilised. The instructor gave me a big thumbs-up which I interpreted as the go-ahead to commence my fall to certain death.

I undertook one last check of my altimeter before sending myself to my fate. The death roll was brought on by punching one of my arms under my chest towards the opposite side. This induces a tumble and spin effect, which leads to a horrifying plummet towards Mother Earth. At that point, I was thinking, 'Why did I let my feet leave Mother Earth?' I loved her, but now, she was about to eat me for breakfast. One second, I saw the plane, next second some piece of the horizon, there was a glimpse of my instructor and then a shed. 'Shit, shit,' I thought. 'Not good. I'm arching the shit out of this. Why am I not going belly to earth?'

After what seemed like a lifetime in a dryer on the spin cycle, the spin slowed. I corrected the spin with an input on my opposite arm. A quick altimeter check was undertaken and I realised I had lost 1000 feet. I had only been on a spin cycle for five seconds, however, it had felt like eternity. 'The boys weren't lying,' I thought. 'That was terrifying.'

My instructor came carving around in front of me. 'Damn,' I thought, 'this guy can fly.' He was looking at me and had a massive grin from ear to ear. He had enjoyed himself observing me nearly plummeting to my death. I took my eyes off the grinning instructor to undertake my altimeter check. Shit, it was time to pull the cord. I then let it rip.

Under the canopy on the finals, my heart was still racing. I flared and landed safely. This time, Mother Earth must have decided that she wasn't that hungry. Collecting my canopy and pack, I began the walk back to the pack shed to find my instructor waiting for me, still laughing.

'You like that?' he asked, with a smile.

I immediately replied, 'Nope, I'm never doing that again.'

Turns out, I was wrong. Again. I did exit into a spin multiple times throughout the course. I even got spun in the pitch-black of night, under night vision. Oh, what fun, the joy of it all. But I do have to say that I am forever grateful to my instructor for making my first tumble a benign jump, because it gave me the confidence to not panic and so regain stability. Essential skills if you wish to avoid plummeting to your death.

\*\*\*

'So far, so good,' I said to myself as I moved towards completion of this course. I had also just put on my third layer of clothing. It was getting colder at height and I was starting to really feel it.

While onboard the aircraft, I felt the heat instead of the cold I was dressed for. Given the high altitude, the aircrew had cranked up the heat so they were comfortable. I wasn't comfortable though, I was now sweating. I was also wearing a mask, as that flying height required us to be under oxygen.

The signal was given to stand up and commence the usual checks. Any thought of this being a glamorous job had definitely been extinguished by this point. It was anything but glamorous moving around an aircraft, with three layers of clothing on, under oxygen, with a bulky parachute and combat equipment.

I think I was about three in line when it was green light for go time. There it was, that hit of cold air to my face I had become very familiar with.

*Crack* went the sound of my canopy opening. What an ever-so-satisfying sound. It always helped momentarily relieve my insatiable appetite for flight.

After conducting my checks, I looked around for my team, however, I couldn't see shit through the 1990s night-vision goggles I had been issued.

I stuffed around for a while, trying to see the members of my team before deciding to follow my instruments to the drop zone. Descending lower, I made out a river.

'Keep the river on your right-hand side and don't cross it,' I remembered being told in the brief.

Instruments are used primarily when flying from high altitudes, however, there is always a chance of them shutting down due to the cold. When this happens, you have to go back to basics, utilising a compass and the land features discussed in the brief.

I checked my altimeter and was surprised to see I had lost a bit of height. Questions started racing through my head faster than the rate I was descending. 'Did I misread it before? When was the last time I checked it?'

Checking my instruments again, that ever so calm, Zen-like voice inside my head said, 'It's ok, Troy, you are going to make it.'

Well, fuck you, Zen-like voice! You were wrong! I checked my instruments again and knew I would not make it. I had been cocky and stupid in listening to that voice and thinking I was going to. I had not picked my out, which is an unplanned drop zone. I should have picked one much higher.

'Shit, shit, shit. This time I'm really in the shit,' I thought as I breathed rapidly, still struggling to find an out. I kept scanning the ground and I finally found a series of small paddocks on a farm. I turned towards them and upon doing so, I flew above some powerlines. 'Stay away from them,' I thought. I really didn't need this already bad day to get worse.

The paddock which was to become my drop zone was about fifty metres by fifty metres. A thick tree line grew on one side and the paddock included cattle yards, powerlines and a row of building structures. I had no idea if I was into the wind or not and at that point, I didn't really care. All I cared about was not ending up entangled in the powerlines.

I jettisoned my pack. 'I'm not having that thing on me if I crash,' I thought. I made a series of low brake turns to wash off some height. Then, once I thought I was low enough, I made what was a noticeably short final. The safest bet seemed to be to head towards the house. As my entry towards earth got closer, I had the sudden realisation that I was going to either hit a shed or slide into one and hit one I did! *Bang* was the noise I heard, as I made contact with the chook shed, going straight through the corrugated piece of iron that had once been the henhouse wall.

Lying on the ground, I took stock of the situation, literally. There were chooks flapping around like crazy, wondering where this alien had come from. I suddenly realised that, once again, something or someone had decided it wasn't my time yet. As I got up, dusting off the chook crap, I started swearing at myself for not having picked my alternative drop zone earlier.

I radioed into the instructors and let them know what had happened and gave them my position. At this point in time, the only questions asked by them was if I was okay? I, however, had a million questions of my own, all aimed at myself.

Carrying my canopy and not much pride, I made my way back to where I jettisoned my pack.

About to descend through the clouds.

'Did it hurt?' My instructor asked me upon his arrival to the crash site.

'Surprisingly not,' I answered.

I was telling the truth; it didn't hurt that much. What was hurt though, was my pride. On jump courses I'm still referred to as the chook-shed guy.'

'Now, listen up lads, don't be like the chook-shed guy.' I can just see it now.

## 20

# Kesh Mesh Khan

'Fuck,' I thought, 'this is not going well. 'First big job of the trip and I had lost my team. As I stepped off the MV-22, I had been blasted by the rotor wash. The sand and dirt hammered my eyes and I was squinting to see where my platoon HQ had gone.

Scanning feverishly through my night vision, I finally found them. I had the same platoon for this trip, but we had new bosses Kilo (medic) and Bear (signal intelligence). My radios were coming to life as I moved towards the team. I had an MQ-9 Reaper locking the target down and an AC-130 gunship covering the landing zone for our insertion. As I reached the team, the boss was receiving a quick set of confirmatory updates from the team commanders. The MQ-9 Reaper reported no disturbance to the pattern of life on our target from insertion. With all the current info at hand, we formed up and commenced our infill.

Arriving in country two weeks prior, this was my second Special Operations rotation. We had done a patrol handover and a few minor jobs in Uruzgan, but this was our first major hit out. Our mission had, however, changed slightly. We were now targeting the drug labs and chemists, countering the narcotics. Chemists were turning poppies into opium and heroin, and this nexus of drugs was fuelling and paying for the logistics of the Taliban. Crazy, how can an extremist Islamic regime use and manufacture drugs for profit? I guess Allah only sees what Allah wants to.

In the weeks prior, Kesh Mesh had been brought up numerous times by the intelligence crew and we knew it to be the fusion and targeting cell. Kesh was a hotbed of activity and had seen some major international drug lords and chemists come through.

Kesh Mesh had previously been hit by Force Element Bravo, which was the military name given to my combined unit. The previous rotation had Brett Wood MG DSM, killed in action when he was taking the fight to the enemy. Brett was a legend in the unit. The senior team commanders from my rotation had served with Brett and were close mates with him on TAG (Tactical Assault Group).

We landed in what we call an off-target insertion. The reasoning was to not alert the drug lords/Taliban so we had the Commando conga line going on for this 20-kilometre stomp in. This walk to the target had us negotiating two mountain ridges. I remember thinking how I did not like off-target insertions.

'Oh great,' I thought, as I crossed the last ridgeline of this hellish walk. I had been talking to my AC-130 when the signals intelligence specialist comes over the net saying the insurgents in the area have the 'green things' out and are watching people walk over the mountain. The mountain we were on was still three kilometres away from our target and we had not been briefed that the Taliban or foreign fighters had night vision.

As we finalised our last movement to ensure the break-in, we came into contact. The boys from the other platoon came under fire. One of them was AT. AT was a known bullet magnet. On previous rotations, he had been shot in his body armour and had also stepped on an IED that did not blow up correctly. The Taliban rounds impacted his weapon and ricocheted onto him. He managed to return fire and, with the help of another operator Mick who unleashed fury on the gun, they dispatched the would-be assailants.

We approached our final assault point. Lined out, it occurred to me how funny this was. I mean, I had an AC-130 covering me, the platoons had been in contact during the infill, but here I was sneaking around for a simultaneous break-in of the objective.

I did not get much time to dwell on the irony of it all, as all hell decided to break loose. The other platoon was amongst it. My counterpart asked for control of the AC-130, to which I gladly obliged. He and Old Spooky (American AC-130 gunship), went to town to regain the initiative and I observed some of the best controls of an aircraft I have ever seen.

As it was really kicking off, the call was made to immediately secure the compounds, to the north and south of the drug labs. The night was lit up with tracers and explosions and I was shitting myself. 'Why does every early job of a rotation have me getting amongst it?' I internally questioned as another loud bang rang in my ears.

*BOOM!* The charge went off, blasting a hole in the wall as the team commanders entered the compound to get a foothold and some protection. While the teams blew in, I was holding a ladder for one of the shooters JD who was providing coverage over the wall. I was in awe of JD. Enemy fire was incoming from everywhere. I was terrified just holding the ladder, but he did not flinch in providing cover. 'Amazing,' I thought.

With the breach made, we all piled into the *quala*. *Quala* is an Afghani house. Traditionally made from mud, these places of residency were solid protection from enemy gunfire.

'You want control of the gunship?' the other platoon's smart-arse combat controller asked me over the radio when things had started to quieten down. He had pretty much used up its ordnance and it was dry. The gunship stayed on until daylight to cover us with its sensors, before returning to base. It had done its job. It helped our unit regain the initiative that we had lost by losing the element of surprise.

'Affirm, ANZAC,' was the call made by the MQ-9 Reaper. 'Two times PID (positive identification) insurgents with weapons digging a device at a crossroad.'

Earlier after the gunship had checked off, I had an MQ-9 Reaper check in on station. I went through my usual process of deconfliction, the friendly manoeuvre groups and passed the mandatory information to the unmanned drone.

'Cleared hot,' was my next call.

'Rifle, thirty seconds,' came the response, which is the call made by the aircraft to inform me that they had released an air-to-surface missile. In this case, an AGM 114 Hellfire.

The teams had all been informed of the strike and scrambled to the relative safety of cover. I say relative, because, no matter what position they chose, they would all stick their heads out like prairie dogs to observe the strike.

*Boom*, came the sound of impact. The reaper called 'good impact', and was waiting for the dust to settle prior to giving us the effects from the missile. 'Looks like a good effect,' came the call.

A standard procedure was to push one or two of the teams forward to physically check the impact and effects. As part of this process, photos are taken. These photos are most certainly not glory shots, but are for evidence. Everything requires a chain of evidence.

Using its sensors to sanitise the area for any further activity, the Reaper provided overwatch as the team moved forward. Upon reaching the strike site, the team reported, 'Good effects and two enemy killed in action (EKIA).'

'What a start to the morning,' I couldn't help but think. It was not even 0800 hours and the unit had a wounded operator from 2nd Commando, an AC-130 had been emptied, IEDs were being laid and there had been multiple gunfights. I wondered what the other half were doing? I wasn't a civilian. I had chosen this. I wanted this and now, this was very real. I took a breather and started to consolidate my radio batteries, food and water. After a massive infill and a very frantic start to the morning, I had not drunk enough water. In the safety of the compound, I checked the batteries on my radio and gulped down some much-needed water.

The morning continued with the teams engaging in sporadic gunfight, protecting the clearance while they blew up the drug labs. Meanwhile, me and the other CCTs continued to work the air.

After lunch, our snipers reported they had eyes on a Taliban commander on the eastern side of the township. Due to his proximity to buildings and possibly civilians, they decided to take the shot rather than use aircraft to engage.

I never heard the shot, what I did hear, however, was the report that they had hit the enemy. It suddenly dawned on me how far away the shooter was when taking that shot.

'That can't be correct,' I thought to myself, 'that shot would have to be three kilometres away.'

'One EKIA,' were the words as my radio came to life.

A team from my sister platoon had been dispatched to provide correlation and a damage assessment.

'WTF?' I swore under my breath. The snipers from Delta Company had just pulled off a shot from 2.8 kilometres!

\*\*\*

My radio burst into life again. It had a habit of doing that. It was late afternoon and the signals intelligence specialist came over the radio. He proceeded to inform me about an area that a senior Taliban commander was using.

I didn't have any of the team's troops in contact so I pushed the Reaper's sensors over the area. I was looking for a needle in a haystack. Giving the time frame and search parameters to the aircraft, I then asked the signal specialist to pass on any further updates or refine coordinates to the area when able.

The search pattern had been going for approximately 20 minutes and I was about to re-task the aircraft when, suddenly, intelligence reported back about a compound with armed personnel. In particular, there was one individual who was standing in an elevated position, pointing in our direction and talking on what looked like a radio.

The area matched where the senior commander was and they were armed, but I wanted to make sure. I asked the signal specialist to report to me every time the enemy commander spoke on the radio. I wanted to correlate this with what the Reaper was watching.

'Talking now,' was the call.

Reaper replied over my air radio that the commander was talking into his radio.

'Gotcha,' I thought, as I began to brief the aircraft for an attack. 'A 500-pound laser-guided bomb should do the trick,' I thought to myself as it was mainly an open compound.

'Got him,' I yelled to my boss as I walked towards my superior. I was thorough in my explanation and briefed the game plan to him.

'Sounds good, let's send it,' came the reply.

'In from the south,' the Reaper called.

'Cleared hot,' I excitedly announced, 'One away twenty seconds'. I had the usual dry mouth and all the doubting questions. It is funny how from the time the bomb is released to the time of impact is relatively short, but always seems like an eternity. There's so much time to think about possible stuff-ups!

'Impact,' called the aircraft.

'No shit,' I thought as I heard the *crump*. For some reason, that seemed louder than the usual 500-pound bomb.

'I think we have had a secondary explosion,' reported the Reaper. 'We will review the tapes.'

'Definitely a secondary explosion,' came the answer in a southern American accent. 'And you now have people movement all over the debris and they are all concentrating in one area.'

'That is strange,' I thought.

'Any radio chatter?' I asked the signals guy.

He responded, 'None at the moment, but we have seen this before. The enemy is only interested in one person. Most likely someone important and our enemy commander.'

The darkness was starting to roll in and no one was talking, so it was our time to leave. Our mission to destroy drug labs had been a success, but I still had a long walk out of the desert to endure.

As we snuck through the Kesh Mesh back alleys, exfiltrating towards our helicopter landing zone, I could feel fatigue kicking in. I had been in this place mentally before and my concentration was lapsing and I was losing situation awareness. I prayed for there to be no hiccups as we proceeded into the *dasht (desert)*.

There's always a fine balance between speed and security, however, we reached our landing zone unscathed and right on time, as the distant bellow of the Marine helicopters came into earshot. It was followed by a crackling over the radio from the helicopters making communication with us.

'Ten minutes out,' came the call.

***

Stepping off the helicopter onto the bitumen in Tarin Kowt, all I could think about was a shower, food and sleep, but just like the saying goes, there is no rest for the wicked. I knew there was still some work to be done before I could be afforded such luxuries. 'Ah well,' I thought. 'That mission really was something else.'

That first mission of 2012 really was something else and some things particularly stood out for me. Helmand province was a different beast. The enemy was a different calibre. There were times when I watched them fire and manoeuvre toward us with separate support from fire elements. I had never seen that, nor heard about that in Uruzgan and Shaw Wali Kot provinces. It had been as though I was watching Aussie troops at home conduct the attack.

The other stand-out for me was how that great Delta Company snipers' 2.8-kilometre kill shot, witnessed by multiple sources, was never reported back home in Australia. I do not know the politics behind it, nor how far it went, but at the time, it was a record-breaking shot. Go figure.

My HQ Team post mission.

Marking for Close air support. The boys exposing themselves to enemy gunfire in order to mark a target for me.

# 21

# A Dangerously Close Day

I should have known the mission was going to be a shit fight. The high fives from the previous regiment rotation as they briefed us on the Afghan village of Peke, should have been a dead giveaway. They told us tall tales of slinging lead and dropping bombs like there was no tomorrow. Now, it was our turn to start flinging the shit.

We were using the US Marine Corps Air Wing for a zerodark hundred insertion, a mixture of MV-22 Osprey tilt rotors, helicopters that could turn into aeroplanes like in Transformers, and the ageing CH-53 Sea Stallions that disconcertingly leaked hydraulic fuel from their ceilings. Completing the helicopter assault force, were AH-1Z Super Cobra and UH-1Y Super Huey Gunships, all fairly bristling with weapons.

The helicopters cranked around me as I sat on the hardstanding of the Bastion Airfield, inhaling deeply the familiar smell of Avtur in the heat of the exhaust. Within the surrounding darkness rendered a luminescent green through our night-vision goggles, we were finally given the thumbs-up by our American loadmaster to embark. Strapping into my usual seat next to the boss and towards the front of the aircraft, I began my visualisation and dry-run rehearsals inside my mind, honing the preparation I'd begun days before. Preparation like memorising the orientation and layout of the village and its surrounding terrain and running through anticipated CAS scenarios until they became like second nature.

Our CH-53 powered up and rattled into the night sky. Listening to the chatter of the pilots as we sped towards our target, I also monitored the commentary coming from the MQ-9 Reaper, already establishing its deadly orbit overhead. JTAC normally runs a minimum of two radios, one for communicating with the ground teams and one for talking to aircraft. Unusually, given that there was a curfew in place, the Reaper was reporting a lot of movement on the ground. Despite this report, the landing zones appeared cleared and I relayed this information to the boss as we continued, inbound.

'One minute!' the loadmaster shouted over the din of the engines.

On hearing this, we readied ourselves for disembarkation with the CH-53 just beginning to power down as we approached the landing zone. Suddenly, the sound of machine-gun fire filled our ears as our tail gunner opened up with a big burst from his machine gun. The aircraft jerked violently as the pilots began their evasive manoeuvres.

Behind their night-vision goggles, I knew the boys were all looking at me like, 'What the hell is going on, Knighty?' as I was the only one that could tell them what was happening outside.

I tried to conceal my concern from the lads, but the Reaper was reporting that the helicopter assault force was drawing significant enemy fire on approach. The Cobras and Super Hueys were going to town on the Taliban positions with the pilots flying aggressively.

Our commander was asked if he still wanted us to insert as the gunships were offering to 'shoot us in'. After the briefest of pauses, the characteristic sound of someone keying a distant microphone clicked in my headset.

'Hell yes, put us in!' announced the commander, with a resounding resolve.

'Troops in contact,' was the call as the team's boots hit the ground running. Miraculously, we had approached and landed, unscathed.

The teams were off, assaulting the Taliban fighters that had presumed to engage us. The enemy broke contact and started to flee, with multiple teams taking chase. Fighting the temptation to join in, I went to ground with the boss, taking over control of the Reaper and advising the gunships that we were now on the ground and all fires had to first go through me. At the same time, I was also frantically trying to battle-track all the teams in order to be able to expedite air support, when it became necessary to mitigate the ever-present spectre of fratricide. Looking back, I realise how vital my ability to multitask really was.

As the morning rolled on, the teams experienced multiple contacts and the evacuation of a wounded interpreter. Things were quiet on the JTAC front, however, that was all about to change.

I had been tracking the teams with an armed Reaper that afforded me a bird's eye view of the area and allowed me to provide running commentary to the boys. The sensor operator reported having a large enemy group positioning to ambush a team, who are not able to get themselves to a better protected location. Electing to engage the target with the Reaper's 500-pound laser-guided bomb, I quickly came up with a brief to authorise the attack. When all requirements were met, I issued the clearance and awaited the bomb.

Every time I pressed the transmit switch on my radio and said, 'Cleared hot,' I would get a dry mouth, a racing heart and that 'I'm about to spew' feeling. This time was no different. Even though I had controlled close air supply in anger many times before, this time, I still had the same questions running through my head, 'Did I pass on the correct enemy position? Is the aircraft looking at what I'm looking at?' And the worst, 'Is it aiming at us?' All my training and the years of effort expended by coalition militaries in standardising procedures to prevent fratricide and civilian casualties are concentrated into that one, very brief moment, every single time.

*Crump* was the jarring sound of the bomb detonating on target, destroying the enemy position and allowing the team to keep moving forward with their assault. Elsewhere, the contacts kept coming as the fight quickly escalated into the heaviest and most intense I had ever witnessed.

The boys received a tip-off that there was a HVI hiding in a nearby compound, so off they went to investigate. Approaching, they came under fire, with lead man D shot in the leg. He was now pinned on the ground, however, he returned fire with his rifle, while continuing to relay target indications over his radio. During lulls in the fight, he attempted to apply a tourniquet to prevent himself from bleeding out.

The situation had just become very personal for me. D and I completed training together. Our families were close and we had shared many barbeques and surf trips together. I needed to control my emotions.

With my mate down, my job was to organise a helicopter, which had been modified to receive, stabilise and transport the wounded to a medical facility, keeping them alive until the necessary surgical care could be provided.

As a pair of F-16s arrived on station, D's team was pinned down by heavy fire, originating from an orchard next to the target compound. The Reaper operator had watched the whole thing go down, so was able to quickly talk the pilots onto the target location which saved precious time. Every weapon has a published distance, inside which a JTAC has to declare 'danger close' when briefing the aircrew. There also has to be an explicit statement that the increased likelihood of friendly casualties has been accepted by the ground commander. I knew that no matter what ordnance I selected for this attack, it was going to be very much danger close.

I quickly decided on a gun run using the F-16's 20-millimetre cannon. While not a very high-yield weapon, I anticipated that it would keep the enemy's heads down long enough for the team to advance and extract D from the kill zone. A further advantage was that if I could have the pilots attack across D's front, I would hopefully be able to prevent him from being hit by any stray, high-explosive rounds.

Everyone's ears prick up when a JTAC transmits, 'Danger close'. As we prepared for the attack, I could hear the trepidation in the pilot's voices, and though over the comms I sounded confident, I was, quite frankly, terrified.

The lead pilot started to falter, stating, 'I'm not comfortable strafing that close to friendlies.' Either I'm a good salesman or the pilot put himself in D's boots, because he finally agreed to the mission and manoeuvred his jet to line up for the attack. Once cleared, the pilot armed up and pulled the trigger, the cannon emitting a supersonic raspberry as the sounds hit home, splintering the trees like they had just been mashed by a giant brush cutter. With the enemy fire now suppressed, the team dashed forward and dragged D back to safety.

Hearing the Black Hawk inbound, I brought the F-16s in for a re-attack, holding them high and clear, ready to sanitise the LZ.

Danger close 500lbs bomb to support the medivac helo. I had to bring in multiple danger close strikes this day.

'Faarrrk,' I suddenly cried out as I watched the inbound Black Hawk overfly the enemy compound! What looked like half the enemy fighters in the entire country of Afghanistan started lighting it up with rocket-propelled grenades and smallarms fire. I was ropeable with the situation now being out of my control and swearing at myself for not having briefed a safer ingress radial. I crossed my fingers and hoped for the best. The crew must have been some of the best because they managed to not be shot down and then serenely placed the bird onto the landing zone.

D was rushed onboard the helicopter while our medic completed the handover to the casualty evacuation team. As the helicopter launched off, for the big hospital in Kandahar, I sheepishly, and perhaps quite redundantly, asked the pilot not to fly out the same way he had come in.

With our fire now directed at the teams from the compound, the orchard and a newly discovered fortified position in a creek line behind both, I used the Reaper to achieve positive identification and it was game on.

All three positions were treated with several 500-pounders, opting for low collateral variants on the compound to reduce the effects on the rest of the village. With several external walls and the roof now collapsed, the teams wanted another crack at the target and so, without further ado, they rolled in.

They entered the terraced orchard above the creek line and as they approached to descend one of the terrace's walls, a concealed enemy fighter opened up on them with an AK-47. W, the team leader, took a round in his thigh. The round tumbled up around his femur, coming to rest in his abdomen. Not only that, but another round had lodged in his ballistic plate and a third had deflected off his ballistic glasses and skirted the inside of his helmet, miraculously not causing damage.

Despite his injury, W moved and placed himself into a position of cover, while the rest of the team, in particular, a shooter KJ pushed forward, with no regard for their own safety and quickly neutralised the threat.

Immediately, I called up another casevac. MT moved forward with the medic to stabilise W. Humping W onto a litter, the team then conducted a full 'man down', breaking contact under heavy fire. I lent a hand by calling in some danger close to the 500-pounders.

'You might want to get your head down prior to impact,' I advised the team.

Medivac about to land.

The arrival of the casevac saw the same Black Hawk crew that had been helping us all day. Approaching land, the bird took fire again, this time from a different area. They overshot the landing zone, flared hard and then threw some sort of bastardised, 180-degree whifferdill turn, making the aircraft appear as if it was an acrobat in the sky gliding back down.

'Did he just get shot down?' I asked myself out loud, with my heart in my mouth.

Fortunately, the pilot radioed through that they were all good and with that, the Black Hawk landed and W was safely whisked away to the land of fresh sheets and hot nurses.

The compound was finally cleared and it proved to be a treasure trove of intelligence and dead enemy fighters. Evening approached, however, the contacts continued. Usually, sensing the pointlessness of continuing, the enemy would, at that point, evaporate into the trees and surrounding civilian population, but no, not this lot.

'Boys, give it a rest!' snarled MT, as he gathered a team and hightailed it up to the steepest hill in the area, to give the upstart fighter the good news. At the landing zone, we wearily boarded our transports, and we were out of there. I sat still in the darkness of the MV-22 hold, physically and mentally drained. I was very glad to be going home.

\*\*\*

Peke was my most defining day as a JTAC. In retrospect, there are so many things I did wrong and so many things I learnt. I still sometimes wake up in a cold sweat, knowing how close I came to losing that crew over the compound.

When I discuss Peke with the 2nd Commando Regiment guys, they tell me I did a great job. Perhaps I'm too much of a perfectionist or maybe, it's the unhealthy rumination about which we've all been subsequently warned, but this day just doesn't sit well with me. Even ten years later, I'm still trying to find a way to stop D and W being hit.

I know I'm resigned to never finding the answer, but of two things I am certain, the American casualty evacuation crew, who landed multiple times on a hot landing zone, are absolute legends and the 2nd Commando operators who, with courage and a complete disregard for their own safety, did whatever it took to help out their mates in trouble. They are the most outstanding individuals I've ever had the pleasure of working with.

## 22

# Mark One Eyeball

*Brrrrpp* was the sound of the M-134. The door gunner positioned next to me had opened fire and the partnered Afghani MI-17 jolted violently while powering up and gaining altitude. We were late on finals and ready to disembark when, suddenly, the flying sequence changed. I watched as some of the operators were launched into various contorted positions inside the aircraft while the minigun continued to spit its fury.

The US had started training Afghan pilots to support the Afghan Government's counternarcotic and counterterrorism operations. The pilots, one American and one Afghani, were highly skilled at flying these Russian machines. Part of the beauty about working with the US Drug enforcement Agency (DEA) Foreign Deployed Advisory Support Teams (FAST) were the support assets.

'RPG, RPG!' came the boss's call over the radio.

I continued to monitor the radio for situational awareness, with the boss looking to me for information. 'What did just happen?' I thought to myself. We were metres from the ground.

Back at Tarin Kowt, we had been on short notice to move, due to a time-sensitive target.

The mission was to hit multiple drug labs in a short space of time. We knew the labs and their chemists were in the area, but we were unsure of the exact locations. That is where the intelligence comes into it. Once the narcotic producers showed themselves, we launched.

Now, we were high in a holding pattern in the aircraft. While airborne, I was receiving updates from the supporting MQ-9 Reaper. There was no movement on target. The boss wanted us back on target immediately, but the aircrew wanted the landing zone soaked with ISR for longer. I knew the boss was getting frustrated.

Also supporting the mission, with the team of 2nd Commando Regiment operators on board, was the Department of State Air Wing's UH-1H Iroquois helicopters. With the mark one eyeball, they somehow had eyed off a Taliban drug lab. It was cooking and armed Taliban security surrounded the lab. The team, who was led by Corporal B, immediately engaged from the helicopter.

The irony of this situation was, that with all the intelligence assets the US had on offer, it took us getting shot off target, an operator in a non-planned holding pattern over a random valley of the western reaches in the Helmand province of Afghanistan, to suddenly spot our drug lab.

Passing the engagement and the drug lab information over the radio to the boss, the decision was easy.

'Put us in!' the boss told the air mission commander.

'Where the hell are we going? I need grid for the aircraft, boss!' I asked, exasperated.

I was frantically trying to gain situational awareness as I had no idea where we were going. It was my job to obtain information to pass onto the aircraft. I had a DEA Aviation asset, a US Marine Corp KC-130 Harvest Hawk and an MQ-9 Reaper in support and they were all asking for updates.

Flying inbound at great speed, the grid was finally passed to me. It seemed like I was the last to know! Everyone was task-saturated and they had seemed to forget about the little old ANZAC call sign. With the power of actually having the grid, I informed the supporting ISR platforms. In my own rough hands with bitten and dirty fingernails, I was frantically poring over my maps.

'Shit!' I swore out loud, before passing on the news to the boss and supporting aircraft. No one had realised that we did not have mapping for the area. 'This is going to be a wild ride,' I thought as the call of, 'Five minutes out!' came from the commander. I was running scenarios through my head like engaging with air support and no mapping. 'Well Troy, they neglected to teach you this on your course.'

Sometimes, fortune favours the bold. Due to the Taliban drug lords being engaged, they began to run and shoot back. Corporal B's team remained airborne, providing commentary on the actions of the Taliban as we landed in a field next to a small village. There was only one area clear enough for the large MI-17s to land and so, we landed second. The operators from the first helicopter were already in contact with the Taliban.

Disembarking, shit was going everywhere. Rounds were flying in both directions, with operators and our partner taking cover and running. The teams from the first helicopter had already begun assaulting up a creek line towards the enemy.

In the melee, I was separated from my HQ element as I frantically ran for cover. I ended up with a combined assault team. We pushed through the width of the village and suddenly came upon the fray of the ongoing contact.

One hundred or so metres away were the chemist's Taliban security team engaging our initial assault team. We had popped out at a different location thus providing the enemy with a problem or conundrum. I fired my weapon and for once, I actually hit the target. I watched an individual, wearing a long blue robe, lifelessly fall to the ground.

Still shot off my helmet cam engaging the Taliban. This one I saw drop or I say, slump.

Did I care? No, I didn't. He had been trying to kill my mates. Now, we started to receive fire in our direction. It makes me laugh when people talk about effective fire and its relative distances. Being shot at sucks and in your mind, an element of self-preservation definitely takes over, but for me, the element of not letting your mates down is far stronger.

Despite my hunger for the fight, I checked my ego. I remembered my primary role and why I was essentially there. 'Troy, you are the air guy,' I said to myself. While I had shot at enemy before, this time, I had witnessed the hit. The way the target had dropped or should I say, slumped. It is still burnt into my eyes, however, not necessarily in a bad way. I did feel proud at that moment. I felt proud that I may have stopped a friend and comrade from being killed.

By no means am I glorifying the reality of battle, but the emotions I felt were different and unexpected. I went on to experience this same feeling many times during this rotation and even at close quarters.

Whilst the aforementioned scenes portray the confusion on insertion, the situation was quickly gripped up. The team commanders took charge issuing orders over the radio and rapidly gained a hold, utilising two key factors. Coordination and retention of the initiative was then needed, and the team commanders provided that. I was in awe of how the situation was acted upon, executed and finalised, just like that. They say no plan survives the first shot, but I was lucky. I had numerous great leaders on the battlefield that day, which, in all honesty, was the standard really.

Picture this, if you will. We had a team of two DEA agents, two shooters from the regiment and myself, but due to our levels of training, we made it happen. In fact, this is the beauty of Special Operations. Every man can think for themselves and is not just a number, however, I myself was getting task-saturated, again. I was part of this combined assault group pushing towards the enemy, plus my aircraft were overhead now and with sensors in the area. I was talking to the boys on the birds and the Reaper and then the gunship also wanted in on the action!

I bounded forward, taking a knee on the hard Afghan rocks. 'Well, that hurt,' I thought to myself as my knee throbbed. Despite what a crusty warrant officer tells you, sometimes 'being on your guts' is not the best option. We were not receiving fire, but the voice traffic from the aircraft had increased significantly. I was maxed out and losing situational awareness at a rapid rate.

With the aircraft pestering me for updates, it was time to regain some awareness and actually do my job. Again, I reminded myself that I was a combat controller providing a role as a JTAC for a Commando element. I yelled out to the team, 'I'm out boys, air is on, get ready for some cleared hot.'

Reality was I did have air on and I was task-saturated. I had learnt there was only so much I could do. I wasn't Batman, hell, I wasn't even Robin. Every person has a limit and controlling multiple aircraft, tracking where teams are and being in a gunfight is mine. I fell out and used a back channel on the radio with the sig to find out where my HQ element was.

Dropping back, I found my HQ element bounding forward behind the assault teams doing their command and control thing.

'Ahh, you're alive,' the boss quipped, smiling.

'Yep, I am back,' I replied half cheekily.

We bounded forward keeping the assault elements in sight, when we suddenly rolled over the top of the enemy I had engaged earlier. The blue robed man laid there lifeless. He was missing part of his head and had multiple wounds to the body.

The dead enemy were checked and weapons unloaded, tossing them aside as the boys continued the pursuit. This was standard. We would later revisit these positions taking photos for our chain of evidence as well as statements, as we were always under a microscope for our actions.

'Got 'em, Boss,' came the call over the radio. The assaulters, along with our Afghan partner force, had pushed through the hail of gunfire and killed not only the chemist, but the final elements of his security detachment.

***

'Knighty, get up here!' was the call from the lead DEA agent. We had dispatched the chemist, security team and now we were moving back up to the original position where the cooking was taking place. 'Oh,' I thought upon reaching the Taliban lab. It was huge, a real witches den for conjuring up their addictive potions. 'How did this valley not come onto our radar?' I couldn't help but ask myself, shaking my head.

Standing on the periphery, I was almost part of a conversation.

'How are we going to destroy this?' I heard someone ask.

That was the common denominator. We had demolition charges but not enough to destroy the place. This laboratory was huge.

The chemist was from another country, allegedly. His security detail commander was someone the UK Special Forces had been chasing for a long time, and here we had stumbled across the lab with the mark one eyeball.

I stepped into the conversation. 'What is up?' I asked.

'Can we blow this up with bombs? We do not have enough demolitions to achieve the job.'

'Yes,' I retorted, 'but, let me get the approval.'

Yep, I still had to get approval. I understand it's one thing to drop bombs when in contact or have hostile intent but to drop on a drug lab with zero chance of civilian casualties, I still needed heaven and earth to move.

I had the US call sign Filth on the radio. I briefed Filth on my intentions and they were only too happy to oblige. In fact, they were on there the whole time, trying to engage. Due to the fact I did not have mapping, was involved in the gunfight myself and maxed out, I didn't let them shoot. This is what I love about the marines, their aggressive can-do attitude. Absolute champions in my eyes and I still owe a great debt of thanks to any US marine, woman or man, who has served their country.

I had a forward-thinking Aussie on the desk, back in Tarin Kowt that day.

'Strike approved,' came the call.

The drug labs weren't something you have seen off the TV series *Breaking Bad*, but instead they are a series of cut down 48-gallon drums with fires and some hessian. God knows what kind of fumes or carcinogenic stuff we inhaled, however, in hindsight, it was probably no worse than the Tarin Kowt shit pit.

I marked the position and relayed the information to Filth.

'Two by hellfire or AGM 114s post your blow or demolition should do the trick,' came the response from the weapon office onboard the aircraft.

'Cleared hot,' I transmitted to the KC-130 while sitting well outside the danger distances.

'Two away 20 seconds,' was the reply.

We had already blown the lab, but true to the experienced DEA guy, we did not destroy it.

*Crump*. With the AGM – 114's impact, came a shudder.

'Ten minutes out,' was the call over the radio from the helicopters.

At this point, I seriously questioned why my life was lived minute by minute? Helicopters were inbound and I still needed a bomb damage assessment (BDA).

'Filth, I need BDA asap, extraction inbound.'

'Roger that, ANZAC, once dust settles, we will provide,' responded Filth.

'One minute,' I heard in my ear from the extraction aircraft. I had visuals on the helicopters and still no bomb damage assessment.

'Stuff it,' the boss said. 'We are getting on those birds. We have blown it up, as best we can.'

I nodded in agreement. It was true. 'What else could we do?' I thought to myself.

We got on the helicopters and while airborne, I received the call that the drug lab target was destroyed.

'Good,' I said thinking how many lives might have been saved without that shit on the streets and without that particular drug money that was funding the Taliban's activities.

Post mission pic the helo. Although I inserted on the Russian built Mi17. Could not pass up a pic with the DOS air wing.

I jumped into the back of the shitty Ford ute that met us at the Tarin Kowt flight line. I noticed my knee was still throbbing. Like normal, I disregarded my knee and I started to reflect, with thoughts racing through my head. I actually thought that what had just happened was pretty freaking ninja and executed in true Special Forces style, my thoughts, however, then turned to home. Things weren't great there.

For a while now, the conversations with my wife had been short and a bit snappy. We could only chat via landline or skype and I would only call every two weeks or so. I loved my wife and especially my five children and when I was away, I wanted to be home. I wanted to be cuddled up to the woman I had married, stroking her hair and seeing her smile, but when I was home, I just wanted to be away again. It didn't make any sense.

## Account of events from Murray Turner

This particular job was one of our Nexus missions, which meant it was a DEA/State Department mission which involved destroying heroin laboratories and neutralising Taliban security attached to the labs.

By this stage, most of the High Value and Mid-level Individuals (HVI, MVIs) were either killed or had fled to Pakistan, but the HVIs in

Pakistan had figured out that the best way to finance the war against the US was to grow and eventually sell the black tar element of heroin. These drug labs had now teamed up with the remaining Taliban to ensure they had the best armed protection of the remaining money maker, being the drugs.

For us, it was a win-win situation. We had the advantage of destroying drug labs and cleaning up the area of the last remaining Taliban. Unlike the early days of hitting the drug labs and having very little resistance, these days it was normally the case that the chance of going kinetic and being involved in heavy firefights was extremely high. That suited us just fine.

This particular helo package involved MI-17 and Huey aircraft, with my platoon divided amongst two MI-17 Russian-built troop carriers and one Huey which contained an assault team. We had a mix of American and Afghan pilots, the latter not being fully certified with night-vision goggles as most of our Nexus missions were day jobs. Any Special Forces units around the world will attest to this as our main advantage, our night fighting skills. If you conduct a day mission in heavy Taliban-occupied territory you better bring your A-game, as well as lots of firepower and that's exactly what these aircraft had, each door had either a M60 machine gun or a rotating six-barrel minigun.

This mission, I was seated up near the right-hand door gunner who was one of the biggest guys I'd ever seen. We had occasionally worked out in the gym together at Tarin Kowt and the size of him made me look like a child next to him. He was American and had been in the US Special Forces before leaving the military and then finding himself back in Afghanistan working for the State Department as a door gunner. He loved the job, the day missions, working out, the great money and he was in charge of an M60 on an MI-17, so what's not to love? Did I mention he loved working out? As his shoulders were about three-foot across, it didn't leave much space in the right-hand door for anything else.

We received the five-minute signal and I passed it down, then the two-minute signal, checking my GPS and making sure my personal assault radio was on. I switched off the helo headset I was wearing and stood up to look out the right window to get an understanding of the battlefield. We were in the second MI-17 and had slowed and started to flare. We were like a low-flying bus, big, cumbersome and slow, about fifty foot up and flying at maybe twenty knots.

I looked out the window past the big guy's shoulders and saw a Taliban stand up about 50 metres off the right flank. He pointed the AK-47 at the aircraft in front of us and jerked the trigger, dumping the whole magazine into the aircraft 75 metres to our direct front.

'Shit,' I thought, 'this is going south really quick.' I desperately tried to point him out to the door gunner, but then I saw him kneel back down and pick up an RPG, stand up and point it at my helicopter. We had now slowed even more, maybe 30 feet up and travelling at 15 knots. Suddenly, the minigun on the left door lit up, filling the aircraft with noise, smoke and the smell of gunpowder.

'That's great,' I immediately thought, 'but what about our guy with the RPG?' Now, I'm tapping the door gunner on his massive shoulders while also trying to get the barrel of my M4 out of his window to engage. The giant door gunner didn't understand what I was trying to do as he hadn't seen the RPG pointed our way. Within a millisecond, the dust around the Taliban fighter engulfed him and I knew, in that moment, he had fired the rocket and at that range, distance and height, I knew this was it, I was going to 'buy the farm' as they call it, in the back of a Russian helicopter, somewhere in Southern Afghanistan. I braced and waited, but there was no impact! He had somehow missed and just as the M60 and my M4 swung around to engage through the right door, he vanished.

We immediately powered up and put the pedal to the metal. Someone above my pay grade had decided that was enough, we had lost the momentum and tactical advantage and we were going to get some height and re-evaluate at about 2000 feet. While discussing options, fuel levels and how close we had just come to eating an RPG, one of the other assets had flown about five kilometres away and spotted a heroin laboratory cooking and occupied by seven to eight Taliban. We immediately reconfigured and headed for that location. On board my aircraft was Troy, the platoon captain and my medic. We landed within a few minutes and we were almost immediately engaged in contact.

Being pretty much the last guy off the helo, I just ran the same way everyone else was running. I followed about 50 metres behind Troy and I could see him taking a knee and engaging targets, 'Far out,' I thought, 'I'd better get up there amongst it as I don't need the JTAC getting more rounds down range than me!' After I did the next tactical bound, I could see him far ahead of me taking cover, changing magazines and then re-engaging a few Taliban about 50 metres to their front. I then witnessed two Taliban drop within a few seconds of each other. It's something about the way people fall that differentiates them taking cover versus being killed upright. Both their bodies went limp and they were dead before they hit the ground, 'Good shooting, Troy' I thought.

Another team commander came on the platoon net and indicated where the lab was. Troy and some other assaulters were clearing the dead bodies, so myself and some other guys followed the DEA agents around the corner and into a small valley where another firefight ensued and two more Taliban were dropped. Looking straight ahead, I was confronted with the biggest lab I'd ever seen. This laboratory included big metal presses, one hundred or so 44-gallon drums and numerous other drug structures.

Troy, our signaller and our captain had all made it to the area and so I called for an immediate brief. We had to understand how long we had the aircraft on station and how long it was going to take to obtain drug samples, plus simultaneously rig up the whole lab for a BIP (blow in place). We had specific and custom backpacks containing drug lab explosives. Due to the size and complexity of this particular lab, we would be on limits as far as enough explosive and also whether we had enough time. The helos were not going back to refuel, instead, they would conduct orbits and come in to extract us on command, ideally in about an hour.

All went reasonably well with the BIP and as we were walking to the extraction point about 500 metres away, the drug lab went high order. Troy then had a discussion with the UAV and extraction aircraft and once again, someone above my pay grade decided to drop some Hellfires onto the target for guaranteed destruction, 'Awesome,' I thought. In my mind, it was better to have slight overkill than leave components that the Taliban can use later on as they find ingenious ways to reuse parts of labs, even after total destruction.

It was now mid-afternoon as we were loading up back on our original MI-17. I was the first guy on the helo, but stayed on the back and counted everyone onboard. I then took the last seat and it was a tight fit as we had quite a successful day. Seven dead enemy and a massive drug laboratory destroyed, equating to tens of millions of dollars of heroin not making it to the streets of Chicago, New York and parts of Europe. Just as our wheels left the ground, I heard the missiles impact the target.

Climbing to 500 feet, I could see the boss, Troy and the pilots all chattering away on the helicopter headsets about something.

'What is going on?' I asked over the platoon internal net.

Troy came back with a response that blew me away, 'Muz, we need a BDA of the two Hellfires that just impacted, we are not landing.'

I was informed the plan was just to hover over the burning lab and photograph using my patrol camera.

'Righto,' I replied, a little bewildered.

As our MI-17 hovered about 100 feet over the burning mess that used to be a well-organised and functioning drug lab, I hung out the back with the medic. The medic was holding my webbing and keeping me stationary and somewhat secure, while I took numerous photos which would apparently prove to higher that these two rather expensive missiles were put to good use. We were flying around in a million-dollars worth of aircraft with UAV, fighter jet and Apache support with integrated high-definition day and infrared night vision capable cameras, but apparently my 300-dollar patrol camera was the go to for the best pictures? Sure, why not?

# 23

# Only in Iraq

Stepping off the plane which had just landed at Baghdad International airport, I was hit by that ever-so-Iraq smell. The smell can only be described as shithole combined with aviation fuel. It was winter and I was greeted by snow, rain and mud. Yes, it snows in Baghdad.

This rotation would see me teaming up with another Commando company nicknamed the Convicts. I had been attached to them while on Tactical Assault Group East and had done training with them. Now it was time to put it to the test.

In late 2014, Iraq was still an internal mess with in-house political fighting and numerous radical extremist groups. The Daesh, which are often referred to as ISIS, ISIL or Islamic State, had emerged as a local offshoot of al Qaeda founded by Abu Musab al Zarqawi in 2004. This offshoot had faded into obscurity for several years after the surge of US troops into Iraq in 2007, however, in 2012/2013, it had begun to reemerge as a real threat. By 2014, this group was in full swing so the Australian Government decided to send a small number of Special Operations guys in, to advise and assist with missions in Iraq. In 2015, I was one of those guys.

I was used to operating outside the wire, and to be blunt, getting shot at. This time though, the JTACs were in the strike cell and this change was indeed most welcome. A strike cell is a special room with TVs, radios and microphones crackling continuously. I had never worked in one of these rooms before, so it was all new and exciting for me. 'Damn, I could get used to this!' I said to myself, as I thought about how the cell was air-conditioned and had a constant supply of hot coffee and snacks.

Another bonus was that I got assigned a room all to myself. JTACs were privy to this because our role required us to be working around the clock. The previous rotation had organised this because of the long hours on the microphone and the concerns for the safety of flights. I made sure most of the operators knew that we had our own rooms and I walked around saying, 'Suck it up boys, being a controller does have its perks.'

I was happy to see my mates from the combat controllers' first rotation. They informed me the role had changed again. I wasn't surprised, you learn rather quickly in the military to be dynamic. The strike cell had moved into the Green Zone in the centre of town and the team had picked up an Iraqi Special Operations force located in the besieged town of Ramadi, located in the Anbar province. Ramadi was a one hour and 30-minute drive away from our location. That is, if one is driving like an Australian normally would. If, however, you drive like the Iraqis do, at the rate of one million miles an hour, the journey would see you get there in less than 60 minutes. Ramadi was a real nice place, the type you put on your bucket list to visit. Not. It was a hotbed of insurgent activity, IEDs, complex attacks and gunfights everywhere. The US base located there got smacked daily.

The handover from the first rotation was standard. It consisted of in-country briefs and intelligence briefs. It came and went. I have to say that the previous rotation flew out of the country rather quickly.

We were keen to meet the Iraqis we would be working alongside. The relationship had only just been formed and the previous rotation hadn't even worked with them. For us, this was new territory.

It was no secret that there was a lot of politics going on at a strategic level. The whole operation was run on the US side by the Army and the Coalition Joint Special Operation Forces (CJSOF), who didn't have their own command structure. Here, however, that was a no go. It was obvious that there were powered political plays with the US Special Forces and the Army.

Due to politics, the strike cell was owned by a conventional unit that came up with a ridiculous strike process, which took up to four hours to release bombs. We were not allowed strike authority or terminal control. We had our own organic ISR, due to the combined US/Australian task force we belonged to. I was allowed to control the ISR to find and fix a target, but once I had done this, I would then have to ring the strike cell and brief up a target to the strike director of the strike cell. The strike director would then have to walk into another room and brief a one-star general who would give the approval or not. Sometimes, the general would want even more information. It was a shit fight.

This shit fight of a process could quickly turn into a shitstorm once I was on another phone to one of two Iraqi JTACs. We only had two Iraqi JTACs working for us. All the others had been killed. These blokes had been trained in the US, back in 2003/2004, when they worked with the US Special Forces.

Phone numbers were exchanged with the Iraqi JTACs as they were soon to be redeployed to Ramadi. The issue of how we would communicate with these guys in Ramadi was discussed and we came up with a cunning plan. We would use 4G! Now, I was used to using encrypted radios and satellite equipment for communication, so this blew my mind! I was stunned but agreed and said, 'Hey, whatever works.'

We used the Viber chat platform for our comms. It wasn't uncommon for me to receive via Viber the message, 'Boom this.' I could hardly contain my laughter when ever I received one. The Iraqi lads always said and wrote boom instead of bomb. Following the receipt of the entertaining message there would be a follow-up phone call and then we would put some ISR overhead to find and fix the target.

I quickly found out that I wasn't the only one with a cheeky sense of humour. The Iraqi boys could hold their own. One of the boys Hussum had just woken up and he wanted to know if I had ISR overhead. 'I do,' I replied. 'I have two, mate. One good bird and one shit one.'

'Ok, give Raed the shit one and me the good one,' Hussum said.

After a couple of months, the frustration with the system in place to release a boom, sorry, bomb, had become too painful to endure. My boss formulated a plan to get the guys in the strike cell to speed-up the process. The boss's plan worked.

The execution of this plan saw both myself and a US. CCT known as JA, move into the strike cell as Special Operation Forces Liaison Officers (SOF LNO). We joined two other Navy SEALs already established in the cell.

The SOF LNO's role was primarily to fight for air and ISR drops for our partner forces. Each morning and night, we would brief the incoming strike-cell shift on what our partner force was doing. Situational awareness was critical. I would link with supporting aircraft via our messenger. The war basically ran on an encrypted messenger-style chat platform.

The Navy SEALs were just as they are portrayed in the movies. Perfectly coiffed hair, muscles that made my own fitness level look more Dad bod than Special Forces and a mouth that ran a hell of a lot faster than my own. In saying this, they were great to work with and the team formed quickly. We set-up a rotating shift system to get to work on dropping more bombs. In between the bomb dropping, the SEAL dudes spent most of their shifts just shit-stirring people on chat or hitting on women, but hey, who am I to judge? JA was a US CCT who looked exactly like Bradley Cooper and I can honestly say he was one of the most genuine and nicest dudes ever. He was a gun CCT and had of course been a college track athlete, so I trained with him a fair bit, trying to keep my body from truly turning into the dreaded Dad bod.

After a gruelling gym work-out, I was walking back to the lines with Bradley Cooper and we noticed one of Saddam's smaller palaces open. Saddam had palaces all over the place from the days of his rule. Being the snoopy soldiers we were, we entered the palace to see what we could find.

'Score!' I said loudly to Bradley, as I laid my eyes upon a golden throne. Bradley spotted the luxurious chair and his eyes lit up.

'We should take this. We can put it in the strike cell.'

Bradley agreed and so the two of us dragged the large chair out of the palace, over to the strike cell and placed it at our desk, much to the amusement of the boys. The experience of sitting in a throne, drinking coffee or my favourite mango lassi and coordinating strikes for a partner force over 100 kilometres away was surreal. Only in Iraq.

Time went on and so did the increase in strikes. The boss's plan had seen a dramatic change from the initial process, but we still had to push harder. My team had to contend with the fact that one of the strike directors was good and one was terrible. By terrible, I mean very risk averse. Being risk averse made it hard for us to do our job, dropping bombs.

Bradley Cooper and I sat down and worked up a plan to speed things up with the strike director. He was known as Flair, and Flair certainly had some flair. He was quite the guy and he was a US Marine Corp F-18 pilot.

Flair was, not surprisingly, all for speeding things up. Plans were being drawn to speak to Iraqi and US generals. Bradley Cooper and I attended the planning process and it was an interesting activity to be a part of. Our Iraqi boys were to conduct a raid to take back the university on the south-western side of town. The only issue was that the easiest and safest way wasn't all that easy or safe. They would have to fight through the southern side of the town. 'Ah well you're in it now, boys,' I thought to myself.

With the morning light, the Iraqis stepped off. Half the Iraqi army was to be involved in this massive operation. Moving into town, they spotted a heavy calibre anti-aircraft weapon pointed in the direction they needed to drive. Air support was immediately requested. I briefed Flair and he briefed the general. It was like a movie cinema in the strike cell, the general was there. Everyone was there. The cell hosted the best seats in the house to watch a little kill TV.

The general wasn't keen on striking yet as the anti-aircraft weapon hadn't fired on our partner force.

'Sir, under our ROE, we can drop on this,' I said to the general.

The general responded to me. 'Tell your boys to move forward. Have it fire on them, then we will strike.'

'Like hell I will!' I snapped back to the high-ranking officer. Order or not, there was no way I was going to advise the unit's partner force to be fired upon and possibly take casualties. Doing such a thing meant that I would lose all credibility with my partner force and inevitably give me years of nightmares.

You could cut the air with a knife in that little cell. The tension was thick, but despite my much lower rank, I wasn't budging.

'Sir, look, we need to stop pissing and start fucking here. My boys will roll in ASAP after you destroy that weapon.'

'Sir, I agree. Hitting is the best option,' Flair piped up.

The general smiled and said, 'Alright, let's hit this thing and start this rock show.'

The order was complied with by the JTACs on the desk, annihilating the target and the Iraqi boys then stepped off.

Picture a scene from the *Wacky Races* cartoon and that is what the initial take-off was like. I saw some shit, sitting there watching the kill TV. Cars and bodies going everywhere. Gunfire going everywhere.

I had Raed on the phone cheering and telling me to, 'Bring more booms, fucker.'

Fucker was Raed's nickname for me. In fact, I think he called everyone that.

Targets came in thick and fast and the JTACs were getting bombs off to the left, right and centre. It was a good start to the counteroffensive and the general, along with his Iraqi counterparts, were sitting back looking happy.

With speed, surprise and violence of action, the Iraqis rolled up to the heavily fortified university. Our intelligence meant that we knew there were multiple anti-aircraft weapons in there. A university is a school and therefore, it was on the Geneva convention list of being a protected item. Places of worship and hospitals are also on this list.

Prior to the operation, we had gone through a drawn-out process called a Cat1 removal. It is a legal process to have that one school revoked from being a protected item for that one operation. A lot of lawyers and evidence needs to be presented for it and I had even given a statement to what I had witnessed.

We were still waiting on this removal to come through, to proceed with the assault. Waiting on this, naturally slowed things down, but the Iraqi boys didn't seem to mind. They got a rest from fighting for a day or so. Finally, the removal came through and it was time to assault the objective.

'Stuff having that job!' I thought to myself as I knew the plan was to ram the gate down with a bulldozer. Apparently, the bulldozer driver must have had the same line of thinking as he was nowhere to be seen!

'*Shway shway,*' they say in Iraq, meaning patience, patience. I know nothing happens quickly in Iraq, but I was running out of *shway,* so I rang Raed.

'Raed, sitrep! What the hell is going on?' I snapped down the phone line.

'The bulldozer driver is not here, but don't worry, fucker, we have a replacement.'

On the screen and out of nowhere, I see this bulldozer appear. It's zigzagging and bouncing up the road, at the slowest speed I've ever witnessed. Turns out the replacement was a volunteer who had only just learnt to drive the thing, ten minutes beforehand.

'Only in Iraq,' I once again said to myself, shaking my head. The trucks rolled into weapons range and instantly received fire from the university. The Iraqi vehicles poured suppressive fire onto the building in order to protect that albeit brave Iraqi soul that was going to try to rip down the gate with his very limited heavy machinery experience.

This comedy unfolding in front of my eyes meant that the Iraqi boys were copping a flogging, which wasn't funny. In fact, it made me angry. I hit Flair and the general up to use CAS and they approved. While a hellfire missile was going through one of the university windows, the dozer driver was still stuffing around. Turns out that on his ten-minute heavy machinery operators licence course, he only got to drive the piece of plant forwards. He didn't know how to put it in reverse or move the bucket around. I can just see his impromptu Iraqi teacher saying to him, 'Don't worry, mate, you'll learn on the job. Piece of piss.'

The dozer driver did learn and the gate was finally ripped down. The Iraqi guys flooded the target. The comedy of errors wasn't over yet, and the dozer driver crashed the machine into the wall of the university. He was okay though and joined in on the fight.

'Bravo,' we cheered from the strike cell, I think I may have even been clapping. I was watching flashes and large explosions everywhere. Luckily, I wasn't epileptic, otherwise, I definitely would have had a fit. Breaching charges on multiple entry points were being used. *Bang*, there goes a wall. *Boom*, there goes a door. Part of me wished I was there with the boy's, shoulder to shoulder, making entry, but then I sipped my warm caramel latte and took a bite of my breakfast doughnut, I reassessed my line of thinking and three words came to mind, 'Fuck that shit'.

The objective was secured and the rest of the Iraqis were starting to roll in. The boys were setting-up camp and preparing for a very well-earned rest. A large amount of useful intelligence was found at the university. The boys' stay became extended because the rest of the assault throughout the town had stalled. Both the Iraqi and the US generals were getting frustrated at the progress of the counteroffensive. I worked with the strike cell for the general, who ran the Combined Joint Operations Cell – Baghdad ( CJOC-B).

TikTok and Instagram weren't around then, so after weeks of boredom, I was over the moon when the general came in and announced he had a plan.

'We are sending in Knighty's Iraqi boys to get this battle moving,' he announced.

I laughed until I realised that he was serious. The general continued, 'They are the ones who only like to fight.'

'Faarrrrk,' I thought. 'Raed and Hussam are going to love this.'

While they weren't my boys, I was kind of chuffed that the general referred to them as my mates. I was proud of them, but they had been fighting for years and would continue to do so. After that initial cut-the-tension-with-a-knife day, the general and I had developed a bit more of a friendship. I like to think I had won his respect. He was a hard-as-nails US Marine Corps infantry officer and this was evident in his everyday life.

'Fucker, you motherfucker, fucking fucker.' came out of Raed and straight in my direction.

I retaliated, 'Hey mate, it's not like I made the plans.'

I understood why Raed was pissed off. The Iraqis were only supposed to be used for that one raid. I think he wanted to get back to Baghdad and spend some time with his children, which I couldn't blame him for. I was a father myself. I missed my children, too.

Hussum was a little more chilled with his response than Raed, 'Give me the good aircraft and Raed the shit one,' he reminded me.

As they pushed into the north of the city, they encountered some heavy fighting and the casualty count wasn't light. Just like clockwork, each day, they pushed on. Every day we pushed on to work the JTAC side and drop more bombs in support of the boys.

By this stage, I had begun to work the actual JTAC desk in order to assist with the Tactical Air Control Party (TACP) who were normally working the microphone. I was working some US F-16s when Raed rang up.

'We are taking fire from a Ferris wheel in an amusement park,' Raed told me down the line.

My ears immediately pricked up, had I heard that correctly? Ferris wheel?

I pushed some ISR over to have a look with its sensors. It was affirmative, it was indeed a Ferris wheel. Flair had moved on from the cell and we had a new strike director Tim.

'Oh, Sir, you have to let me blow this up. This is my dream strike,' I said to Tim, laughing out loud. I continued with my convincing, 'C'mon my Iraqi JTAC is always on the money.'

Tim had replaced Flair as the strike cell director. He was a commonsense US Marine Corps pilot who had similar instincts to his predecessor. He always backed you but stood by his word if he disagreed and always provided sound logic.

Tim took my request to the general and reluctantly (and probably wisely), it was declined.

'Damn it,' I thought when I was informed my request had been rejected. It didn't stop with me though. The Iraqis were bogged down in fighting in that area which meant they were there for some time. Every JTAC rotating on shift would ask me, 'Has your guy been shot at again from the Ferris wheel?' Everyone wanted that target.

# 24

# Human Performance and a Parallel Universe

As a combat controller, I had this amazing physical strength and conditioning coach. They advised me on nutrition, prehabilitation and rehabilitation. As much as I like strength training and making gains, I like mental prehabilitation even more. Wait, did I just create my own phrase in a typical military senior noncommissioned officer way? This is one of those chapters that the nerds should enjoy.

## Critical thinking

What is critical thinking? I am referring to critical thinking in the combat control sense.

For me, it is the power to think and decide, without the bias of emotion, political alliances or beliefs. You analyse, interpret, regulate any emotion, in order to problem-solve and utilise it for situational awareness. Situational awareness is not only for yourself and the supporting aircraft, but the Special Operations team on the ground, the ones you are dropping the bombs for.

This type of thinking starts off slow, but as experience grows, it happens at the speed of light. Conventional leaders in the military often prefer yes-men. Do not get me wrong, the military needs people to follow orders, but a blindly following orders does not always work.

Implemented correctly, critical thinking can be applied in a split-second decision on entering a room and assessing another human as a threat or not. It can apply to non-traditional planning for missions and most certainly is used in the application of air power. For instance, when I was in the Green Team, I had to apply critical thinking. The Green Team is the team in charge of the controllers' pipeline. They take care of screening, selection, reo and the blue pipeline. The other training instructors and I would teach the trainee controllers a baseline way to survey, rack and stack aircraft and shoot. I understood that just because I change a magazine in a certain way does not mean that it works for everyone else.

'Go away and work out your options and then come back and show me,' I would say.

Naturally, the candidate must meet the standards and be safety compliant, but I can understand that someone else's fine motor skills may differ to mine. We are all different. Due to poor leadership and even poorer training regulations, initially, we were not allowed to do this. It was, and still is, hard to break this cycle.

Critical thinking, when dropping or releasing a bomb from an aircraft, is similar. While on deployment, having been in a particular province before and having the shit shot out of me, my initial thoughts were often, 'I want to level this place.' Having a mate killed in that same location would make me want revenge, but I had to take control of my feelings. After analysing and evaluating the situation, without the bias, the decision was made. Do not drop the bomb.

We are all human and experience human emotions. We also experience human errors. I never dropped a bomb on enemy who did not warrant it, but there were a few drops I should have been more aggressive with.

I often think about how If I had gone harder on the munitions and not stuffed around with low collateral bombs, things may have been different. Yeah, yeah, I know, I can't change the past. My psychologist tells me this continuously. I do agree with the doctor, but this directly relates to the theories of critical thinking and problem-solving.

Over time and, with the influence of experienced guys and external training groups, a change came for the better. In my role on the Green Team, I was able to pass on the 'What now? What next?' and 'What ifs?' and dissect the critical thinking process.

Critical thinking revolves more around emotional intelligence than intellectual intelligence. Again, I am no psychologist, but this is an opinion formed after twelve plus years of working in the Special Operations environment and also a number of years of being employed as a bodyguard in high-risk environments.

One has to be able to self-reflective and have an emotional awareness to not only accept your own mistakes but understand what you did correctly. Sometimes, the Australian population suffers from tall poppy syndrome, meaning we are quick to cut each other down for the smallest of errors. Unfortunately, we do that well, here in the Australian military. I however, never experienced the tall poppy syndrome firsthand, but I believe that was only because I worked with the consummate professionals of combat control and the operators from 2nd Commando Regiment.

## Problem-Solving

Critical thinking and problem-solving go hand in hand.

Problem-solving in the air-power worlds looks a little like this.

If I have two aircraft on the same altitude closing at different speeds, what do I do? Okay, maybe I got that phrase off Keanu Reeves from the movie *Speed*. Regardless, what do I do? I problem-solve.

There is an enemy fighter out there shooting at me or the teams I am supporting, what do I do? How do I fix this? I problem-solve.

I have a team in contact fighting for their lives wanting close air support, but I do not know where they are and their proximity to the enemy. What do I do? I problem-solve.

The aforementioned are examples of a qualified combat controller's experiences and on all occasions, they solved the issues at hand.

How do we solve these problems? Well, as any good business trainer or keynote speaker would tell you, you need to prevent the problem.

Guess what, working in Special Operations and combat control does not really allow that on most occasions. This is especially true from an air-integration perspective where it can be a dynamic situation. It is not black and white, most of the time it's grey and there's something like fifty shades of grey. Sometimes we need to regress to progress. In other words, one must go back to the foundations of critical thinking. That and thinking outside the box. If there is nothing in the box, then why stay there?

## Situational Awareness

Situational awareness is the improvement of someone's perception of elements and events, the comprehension of their meaning and the projection of their future status. The act of being aware of everything that is happening around you. It's what now? What next? What if?

If every asset from the team, CCT and aircraft were in their own bubble, what can I do to get everyone into the same bubble? What can I do right now? What should I do next? It becomes contingency planning with the what-if question. What if the bomb did not go where I wanted?

Ah, the bubble. A bubble means you are in your own world. I describe everyone as being in their own bubble. The CCT is in his, the teams are in theirs and the aircraft are in theirs. Plus, the enemy are in theirs. For situational awareness, I want everyone in the same bubble. See diagram 1.

Why is this important? Why should I know where every team, aircraft and any other agency are? Why should they know what I am doing? Why should I know what they are doing?

For combat controllers, it is simple. It's to mitigate the risk or errors and to shorten what is called the kill chain.

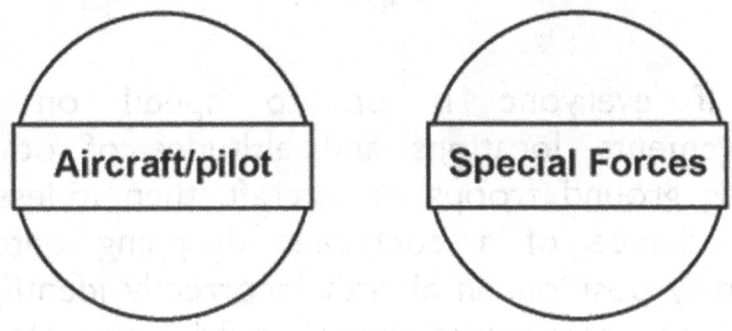

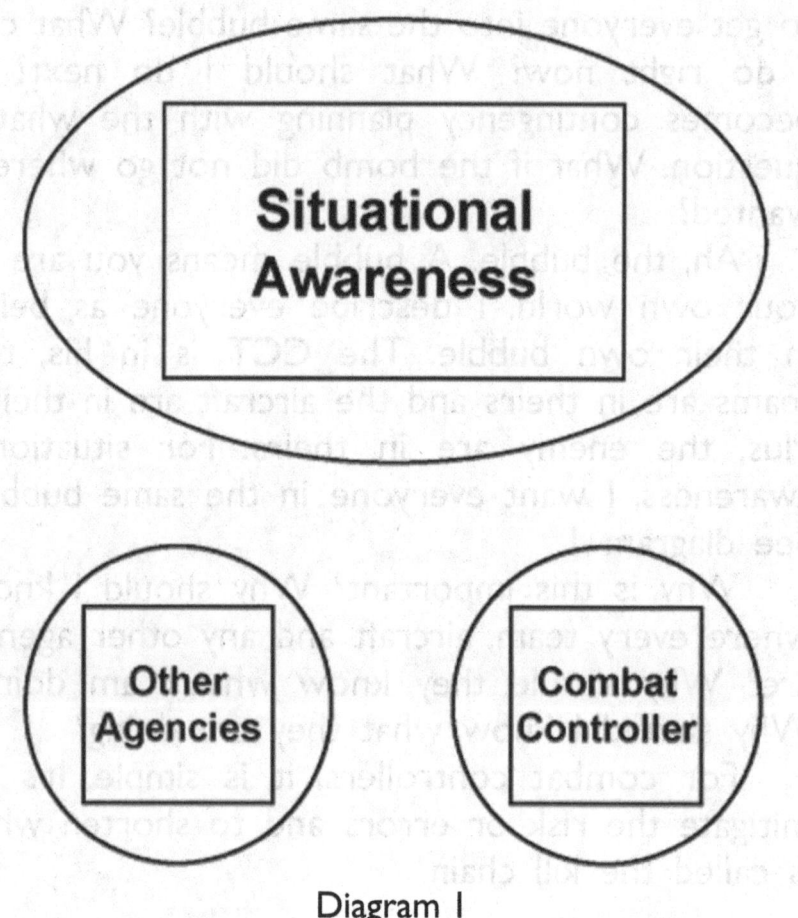

Diagram 1

If everyone is up to speed on the movements, locations and altitudes of others, being ground troops or aircraft, then it lessens the chance of a controller dropping onto a friendly position, an aircraft incorrectly identifying a friendly position as enemy or flying two aircraft into each other.

Communication, I mean quality communication, is the key. I kind of wished I had adopted that in previous relationships. Hmm, hindsight. By providing everyone with the constant, correct and relevant information, the following occurs:

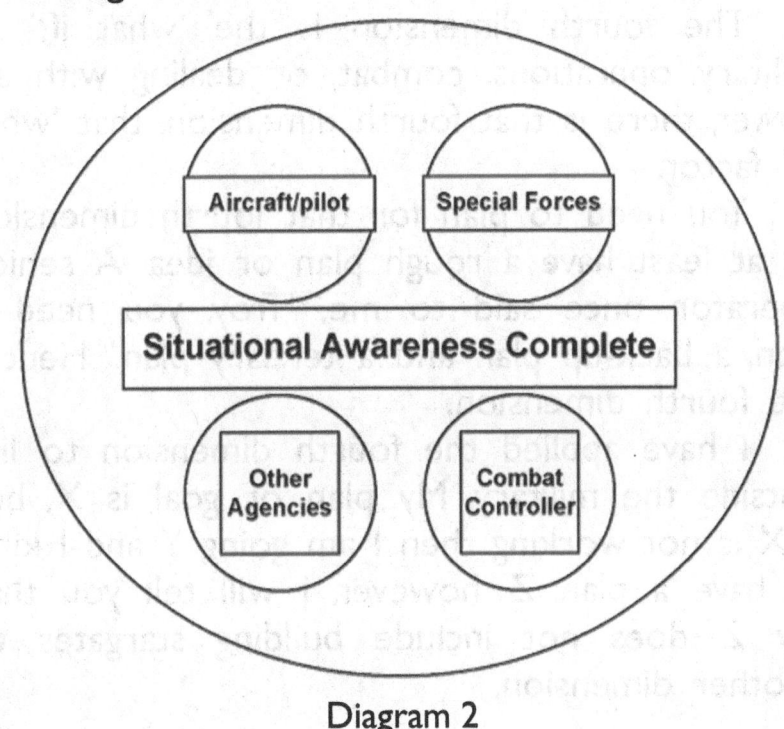

Diagram 2

by providing the constant information and updates, everyone arrives in the situational awareness bubble. This is Communication 101 and decreases the chance of fratricide and increases the chances of neutralising the enemy.

# The fourth dimension

When dealing with aircraft, Combat Controllers work within a three-dimensional space. You all know length, breadth and depth, but what is the fourth dimensional world? What is the fourth dimension in CCT?

The fourth dimension is a parallel dimension.

The fourth dimension is the 'what if?' In military operations, combat, or dealing with air power, there is that fourth dimension, that 'what if?' factor.

You need to plan for that fourth dimension or at least have a rough plan or idea. A senior operator once said to me, 'Troy, you need a plan, a back-up plan and a tertiary plan.' Hence, the fourth dimension.

I have applied the fourth dimension to life outside the military. My plan or goal is X, but if X is not working then I am going Y and I kind of have a plan Z, however, I will tell you that my Z does not include building stargates to another dimension.

## 25

# Welcome to the Jungle

Stepping out of the vehicle, Townsville's heat hits me like a slap in the face. It should not have been unexpected, it was the middle of January and I had been there many times before. I had completed plenty of training activities in the Ville and the Air Force base had been used as our staging point before pushing onto Iraq in 2003. I also didn't mind the local scenery and nightlife, especially the Mad Cow nightclub.

Townsville operates on Fiji time, even the ADF. Don't get me wrong, everybody works hard, it's just that nothing ever happens quickly. Commencing work with the combat survival school, I was happy to find it had a much slower pace than the constant hustle and bustle of deployments that came with being an operational combat controller.

There were a few new instructors at the survival school. Australia does not have the dedicated specialist instructors like the US does. The survival school relies on instructors from all jobs and not only the Air Force but also the Army and Navy. Joining me was BC, a crewman from the 5 Aviation Regiment and JC, an Air Force physical training instructor and BB, a life support fitter from the Air Force.

The first part of our training was instructor development training. This concentrated on expanding our skills and knowledge, plus developing our instructional technique and debriefing styles. Train the trainer stuff.

After an intense theory package of delivering lessons and debriefs, we were off to our jungle sites in preparation for the hands-on permissive or non-combat survival training. Here we would build jungle shelters, start fires, purify water and conduct assessments.

'Welcome to the jungle,' said one of the staff, 'Now, get cracking.'

I don't particularly like the jungle. It's hot, it's wet and everything is trying to kill you. I began to wonder why I even wanted to teach survival skills. Being out in the jungle just surviving was really boring. I much preferred the escape and evade stuff and I was looking forward to that. In the meantime, I just had to survive.

Fellow instructor BC and I were given sites next to each other and so it didn't take long for our shit-stirring to begin. Naturally, I quickly grew bored of collecting firewood and building a shelter, so I decided to venture through the thick jungle and pay BC a visit.

Arriving at BC's survival site, I found he was nowhere to be seen, but I did find a heap of timber for firewood and some longer cut-down trees for shelter construction. I looked at his pile of goodies and did what any good friend and fellow instructor would do, I stole it.

Carrying as much of his quarry as I could, I fought off the stinging, biting things and made my way back to my own jungle site. I threw some of BC's timber on my fire and placed other pieces on my drying rack. When collected from the jungle, the majority of timber is wet, so it is necessary to dry timber prior to throwing onto a fire. Jungle survival priority is all about protection from the elements, so you want a shelter up as soon as possible. Fire can provide protection from the elements with its warmth and it also boils your water, thus, purifying it. Nothing wrong with concurrent activity.

'That was too easy,' I thought to myself, laughing. I couldn't help going back for a second round to collect the timber that I hadn't been able to carry the first time. I was still laughing to myself, as I returned back to BC's survival site to borrow some more wood.

'Knighty, you fuckwit!' I heard BC scream across the jungle. BC had obviously got back before I could take all his timber and realised that his woodpile had been greatly diminished and there could only be one culprit.

I returned to my site, laughing the whole way, however, I was still bored. The mundane survival site creations were not riveting in the least, so I decided to use my imagination and create something totally different. For this, I would need a little more timber. With my machete I set to chopping down a few more trees in the area, plus I needed the extra room.

I mean, why make a basic shelter when I had the resources to create my version of the jungle *Playboy* mansion?

Late afternoon came around and I had this eerie feeling that I was being watched. I noticed the atmosphere had changed. The jungle noises had stopped. 'Troy, you are being paranoid,' I thought. 'Remember, this is a training activity and there are no tigers in Australia.'

It wasn't a tiger, it was BC. What I did not know was that he was stalking me, waiting for the precise time to pounce and exact his revenge. His plan was simple yet effective. He would ambush me with rocks and then steal his timber back.

*Whack* was the sound of the first rock hitting me. I groaned as it had hit me in the ribs and doubled me over. 'What was that?' I thought in shock. Then, like the tiger, BC pounced, bounding in and throwing a few smaller dirt clumps at me. Not knowing what was going on, I retreated to the far side of my survival site.

Gaining my senses, I looked up to see BC with the biggest shit-eating grin on his face. He was retaking what was his. 'And this is for interest,' he said as he kicked over my drying rack.

After fixing up my fire and drying rack, I walked over to BC's survival site. We both laughed at our shenanigans and shared a brew. BC loved the permissive jungle style of survival. It was no secret that I did, I preferred the non-permissive, high-threat side. I was just thankful that having BC near me had made this boring jungle stay a little bit livelier.

'Stuff this,' BC suddenly said, finishing his brew. 'We have done enough. It's stinking hot, let's go to the creek for a swim.'

'Let's do it!' I immediately agreed, happy to be led astray, as it was usually me doing the leading.

We walked to the creek, stripped down to our jocks and jumped in. The cool and fresh creek water was so refreshing and it was exactly what I needed.

Solo jungle survival shelter.

'What are you two doing?' roared a voice from down the creek.

'Morale,' BC replied to the senior instructor.

'Yeah, we are done,' I told him, as I made my way out of the water. 'The union only allows me to work for eight hours a day.' The senior instructor walked off, laughing and shaking his head.

We were to extract ourselves before last light and rendezvous back at our camp. Assessments would be conducted by the qualified instructors at first light the next morning.

Waking up after a solid nine hours is always refreshing. Sleep is a weapon and for some reason, I always slept better out in the bush. I packed up my swag and joined the other instructors as we departed camp and headed back towards our jungle survival sites.

The test of objectives was not so much about the building of our survival sites, but how we would assess and debrief other instructor's sites. 'Boring,' I thought to myself, 'I cannot wait for this to be over.' I just wanted to return home to a cold beer and reset over the weekend before starting on the escape and evasion side of the course.

Finally, we arrived at my site. In all honesty, it was not the greatest site ever set up, but I ticked all the boxes I needed to. It was a little different with its shelter and hammock set-up but seemed to impress the staff with my out-of-the box way of thinking.

That was, everyone but Harry. Harry, the fun police. There's one at every party. Harry was a no-nonsense straight-shooting former regimental sergeant major. He worked as a reservist at the survival school and had a vast knowledge in all thing's survival. Harry enjoyed my creation of a survival site, but he did not take too kindly to me chopping down another half a dozen trees to achieve my outcome. Plus, it was apparently outlined in the orders not to.

Despite the Harry arse-kicking, I passed my assessment of debriefing and basic survival site. I did, however, earn the nickname Chainsaw. I shrugged. 'Could be worse nicknames,' I thought. Funny how I have the most respect for people like Harry. Call a spade a spade.

\*\*\*

'The creek is rising rapidly,' was the response on my radio.

It was the first course that I was instructing, and the students were one of the ADF's finest prized possessions, aircrew. My very first course as a survival instructor and it pisses down. 'Welcome to the jungle, kids,' I felt like saying to the precious cargo.

The permissive or jungle sites sit within walking distance to a creek line. This allows students easy access to water. The course is a training package, with students having had no exposure to these skill sets prior. A beginner's course, as such.

To reach our learning objectives, there is no point making people walk for hours to collect water when you only want to assess them by purifying it. It is a bit like cutting yourself to practise bleeding.

During this course, the torrential rain had already played a factor. Despite contrary belief, it is possible to start a fire out of wet timber. As part of your instructor qualification at the school house, you are required to start a fire with a chunk of log soaked in the creek for 24 hours. I've done it and so have all the other instructors. I won't bore you with the specifics.

The course saw many students not being able to start or keep their fires going. This had instructors going out into the jungle to help and mentor the students through this phase. It was while performing this task I received a call over the radio. 'Chainsaw, grab your students and get back over the creek.'

That's when I found out the creek was rapidly rising and if we didn't leave then, we would all be up shit creek. The voice on the radio instructed, 'Leave all non-essential equipment there and return with your students, immediately.'

I told the student I was with to pack-up his equipment and briefed him about what was going to happen.

Sliding down the embankment, I made a short scurry towards the creek. 'Holy shit,' I thought. The creek was flowing fast and had risen rapidly. I quickly rushed back to my student. I grabbed him and we moved along, picking up all the other students in my group along the way, heading towards our river crossing point. Everyone carries a radio for safety and situations like this and so all of my students were packed up and ready for extraction.

Given the condition of the creek, I stripped off my equipment and did a test run of the crossing, before allowing the students to cross. I was a confident swimmer and understood the dangers of flooded creeks with undertows and debris. At six foot and weighing around 90 kilograms, I wasn't the largest of people, but I thought it would be a good risk-assessment tool to use myself first.

I briefed my senior-ranking student on my plan and informed him on what to do if I happened to get swept away. I jumped into the water, grabbing our crossing rope and made my way across the creek which was now starting to resemble a river. The current was not as bad as it looked, however, it was a little deeper than I expected.

Returning to my team, I briefed them on the situation. 'Anyone who is a weak swimmer or not confident in crossing, please identify yourself now,' I stated. A few students raised their hands. I must have made ten crossings that afternoon, helping students to get to the other side safely.

We evacuated the wet students immediately returning to RAAF Base Townsville where they could dry off and enjoy their ham sandwiches and three-ply toilet paper, whilst the majority of instructors remained at our jungle hut located on the high ground, not enjoying anything in particular.

***

The course tempo is pretty full-on at combat survival, despite the South Pacific timepiece everyone seems to be wearing. The school was running eight courses a year with an Arctic survival course thrown in. Add to that curriculum, instructor development training and courses, it all makes for a busy year. It was a little different for me than for the other instructors posted there.

I was there on a respite posting and to spend some time with my children who I had not seen much of, since separating from my wife. I had struck a deal with my ex-wife to see my children every second weekend and for half of the school holidays.

This deal sounds good in theory and looked good on paper, but I continued to struggle with the father-children relationship. Due to work and travel, in reality, I could only see them for a day and a half every fortnight. Not a lot of time to bond.

Despite the lack of bonding time, I was still enjoying my time at the school and there were plenty of laughs and thankfully, they weren't always laughing at instructor Chainsaw.

At the survival school, we would demonstrate all activities before asking the students to perform them. The first big demonstration was of the jungle survival site. We had a mock survival site made up for a perfect visual representation, with us planning to say to the students, 'See this site, this is exactly how your site should look.'

Beginning at the highest priority of protection from the elements, the instructor conducting the lesson would discuss the finer points of the shelter and then work his way through, clarifying the rest of the camp. He would enlighten everyone on the means and methodology to achieving all things survival.

To prepare this perfect demo site, it takes several hours. As instructors, we would come up to the jungle training area the day before, to prepare all the sites and conduct rehearsals. Team Navy, as we called our Navy instructor, was on preparation duty for the jungle site for this particular course.

Mulling around the helicopter pad after finishing our duties, we suddenly heard screaming coming from the direction of the demo site. Looking over, we noticed a black-greyish plume of smoke rising through the thick, triple-canopy jungle.

We immediately legged it towards the site to find Team Navy trying to put out a fire and it wasn't just a little fire. The whole site was on fire! I stood there shaking my head knowing that the surrounding area probably wouldn't go up, given how wet and green it was and I remembered what a firefighter friend once told me, 'Troy, fighting fires is easy, just put the wet stuff on the hot stuff!' I'm fairly sure she was taking the piss out of me.

The site was completely destroyed by the fire.

'Good one,' was said to Team Navy.

'In twenty years, that site has withstood torrential rain and cyclones, only to be destroyed by you!'

As you can imagine, this gave myself and the other instructors a great deal of amusement. For the rest of his posting at the school, Team Navy would receive a constant ribbing, 'Team Navy, the team that works, sorry, I mean, the team that starts fires.'

It was not all permissive bushcraft. Half the course revolved around escape and evasion. This was the stuff I liked. Students needed to learn what to do if your aircraft had to land or you get shot down in enemy territory. As part of this, instructors have to be up-to-date with the in-theatre evasion techniques and have a high level of training on how to escape.

Aside from running the initial training courses, we also ran advanced continuation training for the flying squadrons. It consisted of refresher training on the survival radio, advance shooting and a refresher on escape techniques.

After one such course the executive officer (XO) thanked me for running the training. As a thank-you gesture, he offered a pax ride (passenger ride) in an F-18 Hornet. I had flown in a Hornet and all the other jets before, so I turned it down and asked if I could offer it to someone else? The XO shot back, 'Troy this is no joy ride. It is an actual training mission for the guys doing their conversion onto the Hornet.'

Now, he has caught my attention. 'Go on,' I said, with interest in my voice.

'We will be tanking for fuel, fighting our way in against red air, dropping live ordnance and then fighting our way out,' he briefed me.

I visualised this in my head and answered, 'Sounds like fun, I am in!'

After attending the morning briefs and orders, it was over to the bunkers to suit up. I already had my flight suit on but had to have the life-support fitters gear us up with our G-suits and helmets. Once fitted, it was back in the vehicle and off to the flight line.

Strapped into the back seat of the dual-seated Hornet, I was listening to the pilot make his radio calls to the air-traffic control tower. He was lined up on the runway and had been given clearance to take off. My pilot was a fighter combat instructor. Like Australia's version of *Top Gun*.

Twenty-thousand plus feet in the air, we joined the other three Hornets. This was to be a four-ship mission with two junior pilots being assessed and under the pump. First stop was to tank gas midair. I had been a passenger on our KC-30 tanker before and I had watched aircraft tank, but this was a first, actually being in the jet being refuelled. It was all sorts of cool, filling up your vehicle at twenty-thousand feet.

After the aircraft had finished tanking, I heard the magic words, 'Fight's on!'

With those two words, we started to manoeuvre into some tactical flying. There was a lot of chatter going on between pilots and the E-7 airborne, early warning and control aircraft. Amongst this radio banter, my pilot talked me through what was happening and told me how to scroll through the computer screens and what they meant. Like almost every Air Force pilot I have met, this guy was God's blueprint for humanity. 'Overachiever much,' I thought, secretly jealous.

'Bandit,' I suddenly heard from amongst the gibberish. At this stage, I was like an infant with an iPad, still pushing buttons trying to figure out my displays on it. In a cool, calm voice, my pilot spoke, informing me we were about to go inverted and dive and then we would roll and level out a few hundred feet above the ground. 'This sounds fun,' I thought to myself preparing for a serious rush.

And a serious rush it was! I do not know what they call that manoeuvre, but man, it's good fun! Something about hurling yourself at the ground at close to a 1000 kilometres an hour is something which I could find addictive. We levelled out at, what I guess to be, a few hundred feet above ground and started a series of hard S-like turns. I wanted to yell out, 'Again, do it again,' but I didn't want to sound like an overexcited teenager.

The whole time, my pilot is casually talking me through the manoeuvres, telling me where the enemy aircraft is and flying this multimillion-dollar asset as if it's nothing. He mentions something about a fox. I don't know what he said about the fox as I was still recovering from my last 7.5G turn. God's blueprint then goes on to explain that he locked onto the enemy aircraft and shot it down with a missile. 'Of course, you did,' I thought to myself.

It was not long before we were back at it, fighting in the sky. This time, the enemy aircraft were onto us and chasing us. I was, however, finally starting to get the hang of it all. I could go into a high-G turn, still listen to the pilot and operate my screens, however, the only thing was, it was getting hot. I found out later that the two-seater Hornet does not have direct air conditioning flowing into the rear seat.

We fought our way onto the target area which was Townsville's high-range bombing area. I had watched live ordnance come off aircraft numerous times, in both training and on operations but never from the cockpit.

It was remarkable to watch the release and impact of the two Mark 82s. The Mark 82 is a 500-pound bomb, which has no guidance system and the moment of both release and impact was another surreal moment for me.

After all jets had weapons released, we fought our way out, in much the same fashion as on the way in. The mission was a success and we all rejoined before calling an end to the activity. For me, the flight finished with a low and slow level pass around Townsville's Magnetic Island. The cherry on top of what had already been a sweet piece of cake.

Returning to earth, I was drenched in sweat. I changed out of my flight gear and returned to the survival school. Whilst still on a high, I felt my body physically starting to crash and I suddenly became very tired and mentally exhausted. 'What a mission!' I said to my tired self. It then suddenly dawned on me that I had only done a two-hour mission, a baby mission compared to other missions. I knew the pilots in Iraq were doing a lot longer time in the sky than that. 'What if I had to eject and evade after this?' I asked myself. I mean, I was spent after two hours of being a passenger. It made me then ask myself, 'What would the pilots be like evading after flying combat missions?' This insight and experience gave me a new appreciation for what the fast-jet guys did. It also gave me a lot to think about in regard to their physical and mental condition for evading, if the unlikely ever happened and they had to eject.

After two years of being a survival instructor, I was missing the combat controller lifestyle. I missed jumping out of planes, running an airfield, dropping bombs and shooting with the boys. I had also had a lot going on personally and in particular, the state of my mental health. When my boss from 4SQN rang me and told me I was returning to the unit, I was thrilled. I had gone through a lot and I just wanted to be home. 'You, beauty,' I thought to myself or so I thought.

Non – Permissive side of survival. Teaching aircrew how to survive, evade, resist and escape. My favourite part of the course.

Solo winter survival site.

# 26

# The Rockstar that Wasn't

I had always wanted to be a rockstar and I do have some musical bones in my body. I'm currently learning Tom Petty's song, 'Free Fallin'' on the guitar. Playing guitar is like writing, a type of therapy and it is much needed.

During my service and even while privately contracting, I thought I was a rockstar, most of the boys did. We looked good with our 'long hair, don't care' attitude. We talked the talk and we walked the walk. We were special and we fucking knew it.

Here's the thing though, it hits hard when you finally come back down to earth and realise that, really, in the scheme of the universe, you are no one. I wasn't famous. No one outside of the units I worked with knew who I was and, essentially, no one cared.

Things had already gone to shit with my wife and it was my fault. I mean, I was never there and when I was, I wasn't exactly the easiest to live with. I was irritable, intolerable and seething with anger.

It was 2015 and I had just returned from Iraq where we had provided advice and assistance to the Iraq Special Forces in their fight against the Daesh. After a long, eight-month rotation with extraordinarily little sleep, I was both physically and mentally drained. I should have been enjoying playing with my children and catching up with friends, except I was constantly confronting emotions that surfaced without reason. One minute, I would be crying over nothing and the next, something as minor as the fridge door being slammed would send me into uncontrollable fits of rage. I had no way of controlling nor understanding my irrational behaviour, so I started searching for the answer in the bottom of a bottle.

2016 rolled around and my workload continued to increase, and so did my drinking. I was the team sergeant for our online team. The online team had the shortest notice to move and was conducting back-to-back training activities without any decompression time. Even though I witnessed this burden taking a heavy toll on my teammates, the job was my passion and I enjoyed the challenge. Friends and family were starting to see my own cracks form, but when concerns were voiced, I deflected them and smugly revelled in my cleverness at having concealed the truth. Knowing what I now know, I absolutely lacked the emotional intelligence required to reflect inwardly on my downward slide.

The first time anyone's concern resonated was during a scotch and cigar evening with the boys. My mentor HR, pulled me aside and made a few pointed observations about my mental health. I don't know what it was about him talking to me so candidly, but what he said made sense and I immediately committed to seeking help.

As I walked into work that Monday, HR's words were running through my head. I knew I had to confront my own preconceptions about the consequences of declaring a mental health condition to Defence. I thought how, even if they kicked me out, I might find a way of dealing with all this unattributed, pent-up anger, but to remain under the Air Force's radar, I was contemplating approaching one of the external organisations that support the military, when I was suddenly called into the boss's office.

Not knowing I was struggling health-wise, the boss gave me a warning for an imminent activity in Darwin and told me to start prepping the team. Relegating my mental state immediately to the back burner, I cracked on with the job, glad to be getting away as I was fighting a lot with my wife. I knew that all my time away and now my unstable mental health had made us grow apart and it was evident we were no longer in love with each other. I was, however, too gutless to end the marriage, justifying my cowardice by claiming I was protecting the children.

The job in Darwin wasn't the most captivating, but there was L. L and I met and quickly I became besotted with her. We had a lot in common and our friendship became intimate. When the exercise finished and the team returned to Newcastle, we refitted and refurbished our equipment and readied ourselves for our next tasking.

I had grown some balls and separated from my wife and this meant I moved into single live-in accommodation on base, where my long-distance relationship with L flourished. As my new relationship grew, so did my mental health issues and alcohol abuse. I found out that a new woman in my life was not the answer to all my problems.

By Christmas 2016, my children had moved to Queensland with their mother and as a doting father of five, this was very hard on me. L and I had been nursing a long-distance relationship for over six months, so we decided it was time for us to live together. I relocated to my own apartment and in the new year, L joined me. I had been promoted to team leader of the Raise, Train and Sustain team, tasked with screening and preparing aspirants for Commando selection, managing the combat control air-integration pipeline and running training activities for the operational combat controllers. On the outside, it looked like I was getting my life back on track, but in reality, I was only sliding further off the rails.

With L now living with me, I couldn't hide my ways from her and she quickly became concerned about my drinking and abhorrent moods. Mid-winter, I participated in a training activity in Darwin for which I was the senior non-commissioned officer in charge of safety. We had worked hard all week, so when Friday night arrived, we unwound with pizza and beers. All was going peacefully until one of the support staff made a smart-arse comment in my direction and I suddenly exploded, the boys having to pull me off the poor guy who had only been joking.

'Knighty, we need to have a chat,' the boss told me the next morning.

I walked into the boss's office where he sat me down and told me straight that he was concerned about my mental state and that he would be sending me home for a psychological evaluation. A wave of shame, embarrassment and regret hit and I broke down in front of him. Then, unexpectedly, I felt relief. Finally, there was nowhere to hide and the entire might of the Defence Force's extensive medical services were at my disposal.

Upon my return, I received full support from 4SQN and the RAAF Williamtown medical team. The chaplain, Chopper even came to see me and, resisting trying to convert a heathen, provided invaluable advice. Chopper and I have been good mates ever since and still catch up for a coffee and a surf, from time to time.

The best thing for me was seeing a private clinical psychologist. She turned me on to the science behind the workings of the brain and explained how mine had been rewired, a result of the decades of combat and other high-adrenaline activities. I followed her treatment plan and the remainder of 2017 passed peacefully. To allow me a break from the high-tempo operations and to spend time with my children, 4SQN arranged for me to be transferred to the Combat Survival Training School in Townsville, that's where I was welcomed to the jungle.

While in Townsville, trying to avoid all the biteys and putting out forest fires, I started my divorce proceedings. I have no idea how to improve it, but the divorce process in Australia is destructive and seems to harm everyone involved. My eldest child shunned me and the little ones seemed to turn against me, as well. The military had taught me to try and solve problems in a structured way, but nothing I tried seemed to work. My anger returned and things began to fall very much apart.

I abused alcohol, rationalising that it was numbing the pain, all the while continuing consultations with my Newcastle-based psychologist via Skype or telephone. The doctor suggested that I might be suffering PTSD, an idea that I immediately shot down in flames. Crying, as she watched me tear myself apart, L pleaded with me to seek further help, to listen to my psychologist and consider medication.

At work, I still somehow managed to maintain the façade of a high-functioning senior non-commissioned officer, but at home, I was coming unstuck. After I had been on a week-long bender, L left. She'd had enough. She had stuck by me for years, but finally, my anger, intolerance and abuse were too much and to protect her own health, she told me she just had to go.

L's departure was a real kick in the guts, but it was also a wakeup call.

'Wake up, Troy, you knob,' I heard inside my head.

I fronted medical again, laying it all on the line and referred myself to rehab, for both depression and alcohol abuse.

\*\*\*

Relieved to have finished rehab and feeling the best I had in many years, I posted back to 4SQN in 2020, eagerly anticipating a fresh start. Enjoying my new-found independence and being back with my mates in the teams, I attended regular check-ups with the psychologist and doctors on base, keeping my demons at bay with yoga, meditation and hard physical training. I remained conceitedly unmedicated, however the doctor was still circling the PTSD question.

During the COVID-19 lockdown in the middle of 2020, I unravelled. A minor disagreement with my boss escalated to the point where I threatened him with violence. After the incident, I went home and just crashed. I couldn't get out of bed and I didn't want to see anyone. I locked myself in the house and I was returned to permanent medical leave.

After hitting rock bottom, I finally accepted the PTSD diagnosis, so I started a program of antidepressants to level my brain out. While everyone at 4SQN wanted me to heal and return to work, I came to the emotional realisation that my military career was over. The job wasn't for me, anymore. Though I had enjoyed the mateship and camaraderie, my desire to serve had evaporated.

Philosophically, I was content that I had achieved everything I had set out to do in the military. I'd had multiple deployments, completed Special Forces selection, trained with the best operators on courses all over the world and satisfying the dream, formed at my grandfather's knee, I experienced combat.

I am no longer on medication and I have a much better understanding of my mental health. It's a tenuous balance and I still occasionally slip off into the darkness. Taking one step at a time, I'm working with not-for-profits in suicide prevention, advising Defence on improvements in their resilience training and mentoring of at-risk kids. I've also started to speak publicly about my journey, to guide the next generation of operators in how to avoid the many pitfalls before them. A way of paying it forward, I guess.

My future seems bright and I'm glad to have found a path that no longer requires me to hurt people. I'm grateful to everyone who has supported me on the road here, my ex-wife L, my mates, my unit and the amazing medical team at Williamtown.

**Sometimes, all it takes is a conversation ... aesh.**

# POSTSCRIPT

# 4SQN: The Origins

To take some time away from these war stories, I feel it is important to discuss where 4 Squadron (4SQN) or Australian Air Force First Special Operations Airmen originated.

I use the term airman as a generic term. Maybe I should use today's term or catchphrase, aviator. Selection for the combat control team is open to anyone serving and I have no doubt it is only a matter of time until we see women serving amongst the selected ranks of combat control.

The unit has evolved over time into its current form. It certainly didn't always look like how it does now. 4 Squadron has an amazing history, dating back to World War I. They were the first Australian aviation unit to specialise in air-to-ground bombing. They utilised the Sopworth Camel to the World War II Australian Boomerang fighter, before moving onto the Kitty Hawk. Enough, however, of the boring history lesson, let's get to the real story.

77 Squadron (77SQN) became home to the ADF's forward air control-variant PC-9 in the late Nineties. The move tightly embedded the forward air control capability more within the operational elements of the tactical fighter group

and saw 77SQN reorganise to incorporate the new forward air control flight, denoted C Flight, 77SQN (CFLT).

The unit utilised the new PC-9 with C Flight-fulfilling missions, such as training army personnel as air combat officers, ground forward air controllers and helicopter foward air controls conducted from the Kiowa in anticipation of the ARH Tiger acquisition. Training Air Force fast-jet aircrew as fast forward air controls (generally conducted from the classic Hornet). Maintaining and developing the legacy slow fixed-wing forward air control capability and supporting close air support training for both the tactical fighter group and strike reconnaissance group bomber aircrew.

The flight comprised four permanent and two reservist pilots and initially constituted the entirety of the ADF's forward air control capability. In an effort to expand that capability, the above mentioned training was instituted, with two courses of four trainees held each year. Unfortunately, due to the pervasive institutional unappreciation for the imminent importance of the role, those trainees subsequently failed to achieve the training required to enable their employment as forward air controls in combat operations. This was something carried over to the combat control capability. We would see the same misgivings and negativity that our US brethren were exposed to in the 1960s and 1970s.

When the ADF FAC capability was in its infancy, it was almost entirely sustained by the passion and commitment of those few fortunate enough to wear the 77SQN PC9/A(F) patch and particularly, by C Flight's two reservists, Dick Coleman and Grant Piper. Coleman and Piper took it as their mission to pass on the FAC torch to their protégés. I'm just so grateful that I've had the opportunity to work with other passionate aviators who had lessons learned and passed down to them. Most of these aviators are either one-star generals and/or international Qantas pilots.

PC9 and pilot flying a sim FAC(A) mission in support of ground troops.

## East Timor

The tenuous state of the ADF FAC capability was brought into sharp relief with the emergence of the East Timorese crisis during the third quarter of 1999. At that time, the only combat-ready forward air controllers were the six C Flight aircrew members and one army controller. Consequently, Headquarters Australian Theatre initially placed all permanent C Flight aircrew on a three-hour notice-to-move to deploy to East Timor as ground FACs embedded with army elements.

Within 24 hours, the direction changed to an order for C Flight to immediately deploy to RAAF Tindal in preparation for airborne FAC (FAC(A)) of 75SQN CAS over Timor. Following a four-week work-up, in anticipation of such operations being opposed by the Indonesian Air Force, C Flight staged a 30-minute notice-to-move operational posture that persisted for the next three months. To this day, there exists very limited knowledge of that deployment and no 77SQN C Flight member has ever been recognised for their service, during that time.

## FACDU is born

Following the East Timorese crisis, Group Captain John Quaife led a sweeping transformation of the tactical fighter and strike reconnaissance groups. Group Captain Quaife identified the inadequate preparedness of the ADF FAC capability and the need for a central focal point for the generation and management of FACs. As a result, working closely with Army, Group Captain Geoff Brown established the forward air control development unit (FACDU) as a standalone entity under 82WG.

The forward air control development unit was tasked with training ADF FACs (both air and ground) and providing CAS training support to ACG. In 2002, Air Force FAC left its 77SQN home for the last time, relocating its personnel and four PC9/A(F) aircraft to the dedicated FACDU headquarters and hangar facilities on RAAF Williamtown.

Throughout those years, now Air Vice Marshal Quaife and Air Marshal Brown remained staunch champions of the cause and were instrumental in ensuring that the ADF possessed a viable FAC capability when the war in Afghanistan began in 2002.

# FAC to JTAC and accreditation with the US

FACDU provided the dedicated focus to work closely with the Army to achieve effective generation and sustainment of the ADF FAC(G) capability. Other key efforts to remediate the capability included the increased throughput of FAC(G) training, an increased PC9/A(F) support to army exercises and training, an alignment with US tactics, techniques and procedures for the conduct of CAS and the standardisation of FAC training with key international partners, during which time, the term FAC(G) was replaced briefly with terminal attack controller and finally, joint terminal attack controller to align with U.S direction.

In 2002, the ADF deployed to Afghanistan as part of the Global War on Terror with FACDU tasked to provide air control training to many deploying Special Operations Command personnel. However, the ADF had no agreement with the US regarding such training at the time and those members were precluded from controlling CAS with US aircraft. To remediate that operational shortfall, FACDU were tasked to conduct a JTAC course for ten Special Operations Command personnel, at short notice, with the aim of achieving JTAC certification to US standards. That training, overseen by a US air support operations squadron, culminated in Kuwait and resulted in the successful qualification of the first ADF personnel to achieve US JTAC accreditation.

FACDU continued to expand its support to the Army with the PC9/A(F) playing a central role as a highly efficient CAS and FAC training platform. By 2005, FACDU was conducting four JTAC courses a year and, in late 2005, became the first non-US JTAC school house to achieve

US accreditation for the provision of JTAC training, an enormous achievement for the ADF.

## FACDU to 4SQN

In 2006, Air Commander Geoff Brown established the special tactics project to further expand the Air Force's integration of air effects into the air-land battle. That project leveraged off FACDU's specialist JTAC and FAC(A) skills and training capability to generate the initial cadre of ADF Combat Control Team personnel.

In 2009, the synergies between FACDU and the Special Tactics Program were harmonised in the reformation of 4 Squadron. The squadron, originally formed in 1917 as an army cooperation unit, was re-established at RAAF Williamtown on the 3 July 2009 and is a most fitting home to ADF FACs and JTACs, comprising separate Flights for FAC(A), JTAC and CCT.

In 2016, 4SQN sought and achieved accreditation by the US to provide FAC(A) training in order to preserve an operational FAC(A) capability in the ADF's ARH Tiger squadrons. Between 2018 and 2019, the PC-9/A(F) was modified to enable the use of night-vision goggles and IZLID infra-red laser pointers for night target marking. It was also equipped with a digitally aided CAS suite to allow JTAC and FAC(A) training using other than voice communications. Made right at the end of its tenure, those upgrades significantly enhanced the

PC9/A(F)'s capabilities in replicating nearly all CAS platforms likely to be encountered by ADF JTACs and FACs.

For a quarter of a century, the PC-9/A(F) played an integral role in the defence of Australia, proudly flown by many ADF FACs and supporting the training of a myriad of JTACs. It entered a well-earned retirement in late 2019, but its legacy persists in its replacement, the 4SQN PC-21. The aircraft, pilots and support staff played a key role in developing Air Force Combat Control.

No doubt I'm biased, but the unit led in developing the way for air-to-ground operations. More bombs were dropped by CCTs in Afghanistan or Iraq than any other Australian Joint Terminal Attack Controller. They rewrote the book on how to run an airfield. They provided the pilots with the required information and with none of the bullshit. They brought air-to-ground operations into the 21st century.

The newer PC-21 which replaced the aging PC-9 fleet at 4SQN RAAF.

# BACK COVER MATERIAL

*I received a target indication from one of the rear team members and observed movement coming from the left of the area of engagement. I then saw them, two enemy fighters moving to a new position. I must have let rip about twenty rounds and not one of the round hit them. I had missed completely!*

\*\*\*

Havoc06 is the call sign of former Australian Combat Controller, Troy Knight. As a Royal Australian Air Force Airfield Defence Guard, Troy had not found the military adventure he sought: combat operations. His thirst for overseas deployment saw him privately contract his services in Iraq and South East Asia, but when he got whiff that the Australian Defence Force was raising a new defence capability, he couldn't help but want to be part of it.

The new Defence capability, termed the 'Special Tactics Project,' would see Troy undertaking the gruelling Commando Selection course and passing, making him one of Australia's first Combat Controllers attached to the Australian Army 2nd Commando Regiment.

As a member of the Special Forces unit, Troy's lifelong dream of taking part in combat operations would come to fruition, but the reality of his dream would also play havoc on his life.

Havoc06 is the untold story of the Australian Combat Controller, but it is also Troy's personal story and one that will resonate with so many.

www.ingramcontent.com/pod-product-compliance
Lightning Source LLC
Chambersburg PA
CBHW010719300426
44115CB00019B/2957